THE WILD BUNCH
AT
ROBBERS ROOST

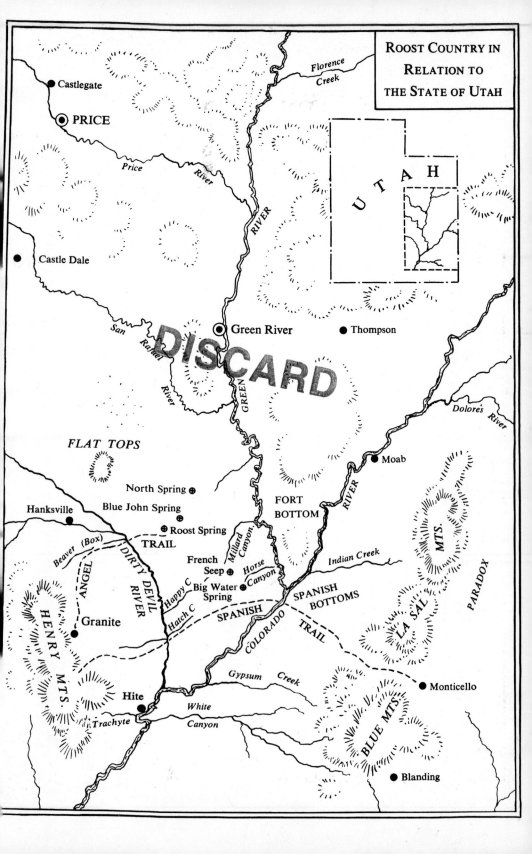

ROOST COUNTRY IN
RELATION TO
THE STATE OF UTAH

Castlegate

PRICE

Florence
Creek

Price   River

UTAH

RIVER

Castle Dale

San Rafael

River

DISCARD

Green River

Thompson

GREEN

Dolores River

FLAT TOPS

North Spring

Blue John Spring

Hanksville

Roost Spring

TRAIL

Moab

FORT
BOTTOM

RIVER

LA SAL MTS.

PARADOX

Beaver (Box)

ANGEL

DIRTY DEVIL RIVER

French
Seep

Millard Canyon

Happy C

Big Water
Spring

Horse
Canyon

Indian Creek

Hatch C

SPANISH

Granite

COLORADO

SPANISH
BOTTOMS

TRAIL

HENRY MTS.

Hite

Gypsum   Creek

Monticello

Trachyte

White
Canyon

BLUE MTS.

Blanding

THE WILD BUNCH
at ROBBERS ROOST

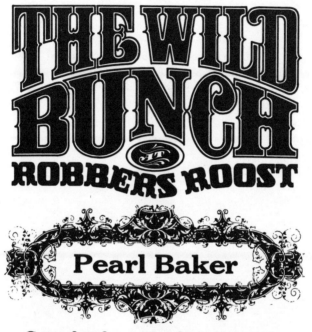

Pearl Baker

**Completely revised and certain
new material added by the author**

ABELARD-SCHUMAN
New York ⟡ Toronto ⟡ London

LONDON	NEW YORK	TORONTO
Abelard-Schuman	Abelard-Schuman	Abelard-Schuman
Limited	Limited	Canada Limited
8 King St. WC2	257 Park Ave. So.	228 Yorkland Blvd.

An Intext Publisher

Printed in the United States of America

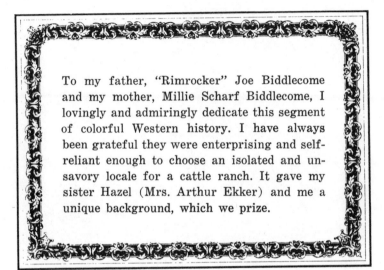

To my father, "Rimrocker" Joe Biddlecome and my mother, Millie Scharf Biddlecome, I lovingly and admiringly dedicate this segment of colorful Western history. I have always been grateful they were enterprising and self-reliant enough to choose an isolated and unsavory locale for a cattle ranch. It gave my sister Hazel (Mrs. Arthur Ekker) and me a unique background, which we prize.

CONTENTS

LIST OF ILLUSTRATIONS

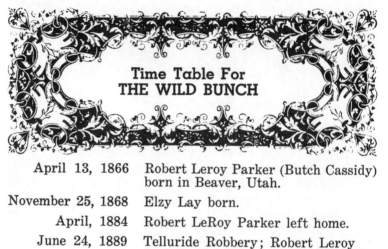

Time Table For
THE WILD BUNCH

April 13, 1866	Robert Leroy Parker (Butch Cassidy) born in Beaver, Utah.
November 25, 1868	Elzy Lay born.
April, 1884	Robert LeRoy Parker left home.
June 24, 1889	Telluride Robbery; Robert Leroy Parker, Matt Warner, Tom McCarty —$21,000.00.
September 7, 1893	Delta Bank Robbery; the McCartys.
July 15, 1894	Butch Cassidy committed to penitentiary at Rawlins, Wyoming.
January 19, 1896	Butch Cassidy released from Wyoming State Penitentiary.
August 13, 1896	Montpelier Bank; Butch Cassidy, Elzy Lay and Bob Meeks—$7,165.00.
April 21, 1897	Castle Gate Payroll; Butch Cassidy, Elzy Lay, with Joe Walker cutting telegraph wire and taking money out of country for them—$8,000.00.
Summer of 1897	Butch Cassidy and Elzy Lay to WS Ranch in New Mexico.
June 27, 1897	Belle Fourche Bank; Kid Curry, Walt Putney, Tom "Peep" O'Day, Indian Billy Roberts.
May 13, 1898	Joe Walker killed.
June 2, 1899	Wilcox Train Robbery; Harvey Logan, Lonny Logan, Flatnose

George, Ben Kilpatrick, The Sundance Kid, Ben Beeson—$8,000.00 and unsigned bills.

July 11, 1899   Colorado Southern; Sam Ketchum, Elzy Lay, Kid Curry—$30,000.00

October 10, 1899   Elzy Lay to New Mexico Territorial Prison.

January 21, 1900   Matt Warner released from Utah State Penitentiary.

August 29, 1900   Tipton, Wyoming Train Robbery; Butch Cassidy, The Sundance Kid, Harvey Logan, Ken Kilpatrick, Laura Bullion and Ben Beeson— $50.45 or $55,000.00?

September 19, 1900   Winnemucca, Nevada Bank Robbery; Butch Cassidy, The Sundance Kid, and Bill Carver—$30,000.00.

July 3, 1901   Wagner, Montana Train Robbery; Butch Cassidy, Kid Curry, The Sundance Kid—$45,000.00.

February 20, 1902   Butch Cassidy, The Sundance Kid and Etta Place to South America.

January 10, 1906   Elzy Lay pardoned.

March, 1906   Bank Robbery in Mercedes, Province San Luis, Argentina; Butch Cassidy, The Sundance Kid, Kid Curry and Etta Place.

1909   Aramayo Payroll held up; battle at San Vicente, Bolivia.

1909   Harvey Logan, killed by wild mule in South America.

1925   Butch Cassidy came home to Circleville, Utah for visit.

November 10, 1934   Elzy Lay died in Los Angeles.

1943-1944   Butch Cassidy died, probably in California or Washington.

Looking down into Millard Canyon from the overlook near French Seep, facing north, the Spur country on the left and North Point on the right. The Wild Bunch often dropped down the rockslide into Millard, and then to the Green River above Anderson Bottom, or off the south side of North Point down the North Trail to Under the Ledge; and finally either across the Spanish Trail, or around through Sunset Pass to Poison Springs Canyon and out by the Henry Mountains, or around the Andy Miller country and out by Hite.

—PHOTO COURTESY OF PARKER HAMILTON, FLAGSTAFF, ARIZONA

ROBBERS
ROOST
COUNTRY

That high desert country in southeastern Utah, around the heads of the canyons draining into the Green and Colorado rivers on the east and south, and above the Dirty Devil River on the west, had been called Robbers Roost * long before Butch Cassidy drove his stolen horses there in 1884. Over ten years before, Cap Brown had found sanctuary there.

Cap was a notorious horse thief of the 1870s, who raided western Utah for horses to supply the demand at the mines in Colorado. He traveled the route a good many times from the Sevier, down through Rabbit Valley and into Hanksville (called Grays Valley then), across Burr Desert, down Beaver Box, across the Dirty Devil and out the Angel Trail onto the Roost. He was probably the first to hold horses on the grassy Roost Flats, and likely built the corrals on Twin Corral Flats that gave that area its name.

---

* The name Robbers Roost has never been written with an apostrophe as far as I have been able to trace it.

It is amazing that all of the trails used by the Wild Bunch (and Cap before them) are in use today, and that they are the only routes threading the canyon mazes. With the exception of a few out-of-the-way grazing areas, such as the Bull Pasture, Sam's Mesa Canyon and Twin Corral Box, the trails ridden today are those laid out by the men who rode swiftly away from the main highways—looking back.

Cap had led a busy life. Sometimes he did his own stealing, but often he picked up a bunch of good horses gathered by someone like Mike Cassidy and his crew on the Marshall ranch. He always rode into the country alone, getting his crew of three or four men at the same time he gathered the horses. Helpers he could have had by the dozens, youngsters who longed to leave their pioneer-poor homes for the rich mines of Colorado, but he held his crew to three or four. When the trail was bad, stormy or beset by angry ranchers, he often put one of the boys on the little bell mare to lead. Thus he could have the herd really head out, or hold back for weak ones or colts.

Finally his operations became too expensive, and a posse of ranchers followed him. Cap had noted the posse's dust cloud behind in the late afternoon as he crossed the Buhr Flats. When his horses had made Beaver Box and dropped into the narrow canyon, Cap and the two young fellows with him fell back in the rocks on the sides of the canyon to stop the posse. The lead man, riding his own horse, was left with the herd.

Cap cursed his luck. There was no way he could give the posse the slip, and if they decided to stay through the night, he didn't fancy a running battle up the exposed slopes of the Angel Trail. He might make it too hot for them to stick around, and that seemed to be the best plan of action. Calling the two youngsters to him, he gave them strict orders that no one was to shoot to kill, but to put the opening shots close enough to turn back the pursuers. He wished it was a little earlier; dusk was just settling in.

At the first volley from the canyon rims, the posse hit the ground, not knowing Cap's orders. They turned their horses loose and started them up the canyon, a couple of the men going along to catch and hold the mounts out of range of the battle.

It was almost dark, and after a few shots at the side-hills, the posse gathered together. In a low-voiced confer-ence they decided to go back home, while the going was good. While winding up the canyon, through the brush, catfooting back to their stamping horses, one of the posse looked back. Thinking he saw a figure crawling from be-hind one of the rocks on the hillside, he chanced a snap shot. It was enough; one of the youngsters with Cap was hit in the thigh.

While the posse mounted up and pounded up the canyon a good deal faster than they had ventured down, Cap sidled along the talus slope to his wounded rider.

"How bad you hit, boy?" he inquired.

"Bad enough, but it don't seem to be bleeding much."

Cap squatted down and examined the deep flesh wound halfway between the hip and knee. When his match burned out, he said, "It's on the outside of your leg. I think you can still ride. But we better not camp here on the river tonight like we usually do. We can't risk it. Moon will be up pretty soon, and we better go right on to the Roost before you stiffen up and can't ride."

Overtaking the horses, Cap put the lead man on the bell mare. Crossing the river, they started up the rocky intri-cacies of the Angel Trail, named that by Cap, who in-sisted it took wings to get over it.

The loose horses (Cap had managed only about forty head this trip) were slipping on the bulging red slickrocks, losing hair and hide, the smell of burned hooves pungent on the night air. The wise old saddle horses, after the riders dismounted to lead them up the steep slopes of naked sandstone, hung back on the bridle reins, bracing and balancing themselves for the difficult climbs. Many of these steep pitches over and around which the trail snaked led down to a drop-off into a black canyon, so it behooved a man to climb fast and expertly and give a horse all the help he could.

Sometimes the leader could find a few handfuls of sand in a depression in the rocks and throw it up on the trail to

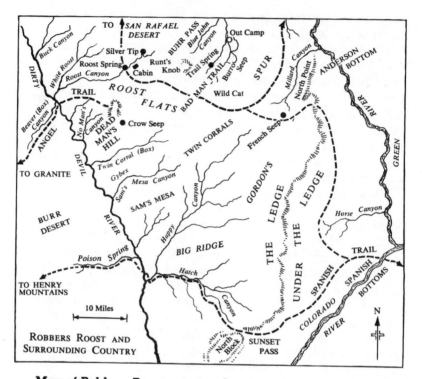

Map of Robbers Roost country showing relation to surrounding towns.

give the horses' hooves a little purchase. The trail wound over the canyon walls and around rims clearly visible in the bright moonlight, but there were places where the snorting horses smelled out the way in the dense blackness of ledge shadow.

The wounded man dropped back, no longer able to steady his horse on the trail or—weak from shock and loss of blood—to climb the worst places unaided. Cap and the other rider waited for him. Cap turned the saddle horses of the two boys into the bunch and left the young fellows to make their way up the trail afoot. He told them it wasn't far and that he would wait on top with their horses. When they finally climbed out on top, he was waiting and told them where to find the camp.

Looking off the end of Angel Trail Point across the Dirty Devil
River with the Henry Mountains in the background.

—PHOTO COURTESY OF PARKER HAMILTON, FLAGSTAFF, ARIZONA

Daylight was just beginning to show when the two boys
rode into camp, in a blind draw near what was to become
known as Dead Man's Hill. They dismounted, and the
wounded boy dragged himself to a bed roll.

When Cap had settled the horses to graze in the Roost
Flats, and returned to camp shortly after sunup, he gave
the boy what rough first aid he could. Cutting away the
pants leg, stiff with dried blood, he found the wound was
far worse than he had thought. The leg was badly swollen,
the boy had lost a lot of blood and was far gone in shock.
By noon, Cap knew there wasn't much hope for him. The
young fellow died that night. He was buried somewhere
near Dead Man's Hill, bestowing that name on the prominent landmark.

After delivering his horses at Telluride, Cap returned
to Hanksville, where he had a shack in Bull Valley. It
was there that Butch Cassidy found him in the spring of
1884.

BUTCH CASSIDY
FINDS THE ROOST

The May sun was just going down behind the mountains above Kingston Canyon when Robert LeRoy Parker swung up the canyon on his race mare, Bess. The two men holding the horses bunched in the head of the canyon, looked at each other meaningfully.

"Here he comes," one of them spoke, "I was afraid he'd let his mother talk him out of it. Funny he insisted on telling her goodbye."

"Well, we could have turned the horses back on the range, and no one would have been any the wiser. I'm not sure I like this way of doing things."

"Having that eighteen-year-old kid drive these horses to Telluride, and then us show up and collect? Hell, Fred, how can you miss? Safe, ain't it?"

"Okay, have it your way. You don't have to go part way with him; I do."

"You only have to go through Rabbit Valley. Stay in the lead of the bunch, and if things get rough pull your freight. If there is any posse business, it will come about

when the horses are going through there, and it will come
from behind. Bob can handle the bunch easy until he gets
to Gray's Valley, and Cap will help him on through the
rough country."

By that time the boy had ridden close enough to hear
them, and the two turned to him. One of them raised his
hand in salute and rode off down the canyon. The other
man looked at Bob.

Fred liked what he saw. He had always approved of this
big, competent youngster. Mike Cassidy, before he'd had
to pull out for Mexico, had said that young Bob Parker
was already a man—a man to ride the river with.

"Now, Bob," said Fred. "I'll ride lead and you string the
bunch out behind me. Keep them close-herded and at a
good swinging trot. They'll learn to travel in a bunch
pretty fast that way. We'll drop over into Grass Valley,
and cross the summit by Fish Lake down into Rabbit
Valley. From there on, you've got it made, until you get to
Gray's Valley. Cap Brown will take you from there across
the Roost country.

"This is about the right size bunch; more than twenty
head you couldn't handle alone. By the time we hit Rabbit
Valley they'll be trail-broke. All right, boy, start 'em out
—and fan 'em right along."

They traveled fast and far that night, stopping toward
morning in the edge of Grass Valley to rest and graze the
horses. Bob was glad Bess' colt had been born early, and
was sturdy and high-strung. The little fellow was tired,
but game, and was still following right up with the mare.

The next forenoon the string topped the summit. An old
rangy buckskin had stepped out as leader, and when the rest
of the horses were following him easily there was no longer
a need for a man ahead. Fred turned aside and let the
horses pass him, waiting for Bob to range alongside.

"She's all yours, son," he said. "They trail-broke fine.
Just keep 'em together—and when you travel, *travel*.
Then when you let 'em stop, they'll graze and rest."

Feed was good along the river bottoms, and Bob lazed
along, just keeping the horses headed in the right direction. When he put the refreshed animals on the trail the

fourth day from home, they strung out behind the buckskin and covered ground. He camped that night near what
was later to be called Fruita, and the next night made it
to Gray's Valley. The next lap was to Cap Brown's.

After camping that night at the mouth of Beaver Box,
the two men, leading their mounts and following the
horses and a pack mule, topped out onto Robbers Roost on
the tip of the long Angel Point shortly after noon. Coming
out of the canyons where the May sun bounced shafts of
light off the ledges and shoulders of the trail, the cool,
high-country breeze felt good as it dried the sweat on men
and horses. The horses scattered across the narrow gravel
point, picking at the short grass and hunting soft places

**Saddle horses belonging to Arthur Ekker, present owner of
Robbers Roost, at the water pond at the Headquarters at Crow
Seep, eight miles south of Robbers Roost Spring.**

—PHOTO COURTESY OF PARKER HAMILTON, FLAGSTAFF, ARIZONA

to roll in. The two men leaned against their mounts and drew in deep breaths, recovering from the last hard climb.

Bob Parker, who in later years was to become the notorious Butch Cassidy and know this country well, looked around. He was standing on a flat, narrow point shoved out into the maze of canyons, buttes, mesas and rounded sandrock slopes of the rough Dirty Devil gorge. Highly colored reds predominated, shading from a sunburned tan to a plum-stained umber. His sight was eased with areas of yellow ranging from the tawny orange of the deeps to bands of creamy white near the tops of the mesas. Their level limestone crowns showed black in the reds and creams of the lower-dropping sandstone.

Across the canyon to the west, five miles or so, a purple desert, broken somewhat by long, easy ridges and open swales, rose from the western canyon rim southwestward toward the sharply cut peaks of the Henry Mountains, blued brightly by the clear distance. To the right of this range of mountains, and far behind them, across the purpled canyons of Capitol Reef and the north-stretching San Rafael Swell, floated the hazy bulk of the Thousand Lake Mountains. Far beyond them, in central Utah, lay Circleville and the Sevier River, the boy's home—which he doubted he would ever see again.

Throwing off his moodiness, he faced east and looked to where orange-toned, sandy ridges, dotted with green-black cedars, rose beyond broken country of a rich dark red and lifted to the horizon. On the north side of Angel Point, Roost Canyon and its tributaries lay at his feet, while on the south side, canyons rough and unnamed cut back into grassy flats.

Giving the youth time to orient himself, Cap Brown rolled a smoke. His beat-up hat, battered clothing and run-over boots proclaimed him a real hand, experienced and wise. He spoke.

"I'm always glad to git that climb behind me. Not so bad going down, but hauling a horse up them steep slick-rock slopes about takes it out of a man."

"Sure does," the younger man answered. "I see why you call it the *Angel* Trail."

Here was a hand, too, in every shade of meaning. He was not overly tall, but he carried himself with ease and quickness. Dressed in the rough cotton shirt and woolen trousers of the cowboy, his scarred leather chaps hung low on his lithe hips, the bottom edges brushing the rough, worn boots. A gun swung in a holster on his hip, held by a wide belt with cartridges in the loops. Typical he might have been of the average cowboy of the late 1880's, but there was nothing commonplace about his intelligent face, usually split by a broad grin of humor and friendliness.

Life had been far from easy in the frontier Mormon family he had left in Circleville. The eldest son of a large family, he had held a man's place, taking care of the livestock and doing rough, hard work on the ranch as long as he could remember. And he longed for wider horizons.

Pushing his hat back from his white, untanned forehead, he lifted his arms away from his sweaty body to let the breeze cool his coarse homespun shirt while he turned his tanned face into the breath of air to enjoy the freshness. A grin creased his round, heavy-jawed face, crinkling the squint wrinkles deeper around his blue eyes.

"This country sure gets under your skin." His wave took in the vivid world.

"It sure does," Cap agreed, remembering the times he had come back to it, homesick for its rich color and form when he'd tried to live in lands less bold. "Ready to roll?"

They swung up and hazed the horses into a smart trot up the point. Rounding the head of a little canyon, they bore due east toward the skyline. The breeze had died, and the midday sun burned into Bob's back through his shirt. The red dust kicked up by the band of horses settled on him in a choking cloud.

Plodding up the last, easy slope around the northern end of the prominent Dead Man's Hill, the horses dropped down the eastern side, grabbing hungrily at the lush sandgrass as they went. Bob pulled up on the ridge to look around.

It was almost as he had pictured it. The long, gentle swales, headed by the cedar ridges which encircled the southern end of Roost Flats, flowed north to the broken drainage draw at the northern boundary. He judged he was looking about six miles across the width of the flats to the roughs of Horseshoe Canyon, beyond which the High Spur country rose, showing some detail of ridges and flats. Farther off lay the misty canyonland of the Green River, and away beyond the La Sal Mountains dimly etched the horizon. Around the southern end of these he would travel in a couple of weeks, and it looked a long way, he thought.

Bringing his gaze back to the Roost, he swept it from the far ridge on the south, down the length of the rolling flats, clothed now in the fresh green of early spring, to where they joined the deeply cleft Roost Draw. The low ridge on the north side, cedar tipped, stretched back into the red sand desert far to the north. This wonderful range of lush grass and early flowers seemed to lie at the top of the world, with canyons draining away on every side.

He touched spurs to his mount and overtook the loitering horses, heading them down the ridge. In the bottom of the first swale, they picked up a trail and headed north on it, following Cap closely.

Breasting a sand dune across the draw, the little cavalcade rounded a turn and came upon two cedars in the swale. Three old steers jumped up, watched the man-enemy incredulously for a few seconds, then broke wildly up through the sand hills. Bob remembered he had heard that a fellow had turned two hundred head of steers loose at the Roost a few years before, but had been able to gather only part of them the next year. He surmised these three were some of them.

A few hundred yards farther the horses climbed out of the sand onto red slickrock, and the boy saw trails cut four to six inches deep in the solid rock. He was surprised for a moment, but grinned as he thought of the untold centuries this land had remained pretty much the same. And the good grazing he was finding must have nourished game from time unremembered.

At last the faintly sulphurous odor of the gypsum-impregnated Roost Spring wafted up, and the thirsty horses quickened their gait. After winding between small rock buttes and through sharp gullies, they dropped into a rocky side draw and descended steeply into the main draw—and the future Butch Cassidy saw the Roost Spring for the first time.

The horses crossed the main draw and swung out over the lift of the hill, beyond which lay a flat place in the narrowing canyon. Cap designated this as "bunch ground." Bob nodded, and coughed at the sharpness of the bitter gypsum in the dust.

A trickle of water ran down the gully, but it was too shallow for the horses to drink from, and they followed around the edge of a little ledge and dropped down to a pool under the southern canyon wall. From the pool, the north bank pitched up steeply to the level of the open flat they had skirted. This bank held a tangle of grasses and rushes from which a sizable spring ran down into the catch-pool. This water, in years to come, would be fenced in and gathered into a shallow V-trough to be carried into long, wooden troughs under the ledge. Now it made its own furrow, with green rushes and wild rose bushes choking its course. Two small cottonwoods had taken root above the spring, lending the clean rustle of new leaves to the quiet scene.

Bob stepped off his horse and slipped the bridle, looking around as he let the animal drink its fill of the faintly bitter mineralized water. The scene appeared as new and untouched by man as on the first morning of Creation; he was to learn in the years to come that the springs in this desert country always carried that primitive feeling.

Resting here in the shade of the ledge while his horses drank, his active mind ranged over his situation. Past was the hard, dull ranch life. He was on his way to the booming mining camp of Telluride, Colorado, and he planned never to return. He looked across the pool at Cap Brown.

Bob had known the old horse thief for several years, ever since he had stolen herds of horses in western Utah and brought them to the Roost. Cap and Mike Cassidy had been good friends, and he had usually stayed overnight at the Marshall ranch near Circleville while choosing horses for a raid. Bob had listened avidly to the two men as they talked in the argot of the stockman "a little on the rustle," with their opinions always colored by the best way to handle livestock fast, and turn it to a quick profit.

The horses had filled up now, and the blaze-faced sorrel started pawing the water while the ornery little pack mule was threatening to roll. Bob bridled his horse and swung into the saddle, helping Cap haze the horses up out of the spring-wet wash onto the bunch ground. Gypsum dust swirled up again as they jogged up the draw toward the east.

The men hadn't drunk the bitter Roost water, loaded with gypsum, but waited until they could get sweet water a mile or so above the spring, in one of the short side canyons on the north.

After leaving the bunch ground and crossing the main channel, the cavalcade came out into a level, brushy flat of six or eight acres, where the sides of the wash fell back. The north side was rimmed by a rocky ridge, but the ledges on the south soon gave way to a high sandhill, its improbable steepness staked in place by low bushes and grass.

Among the brush in the flat bottom, trails wound, marked by cattle use. After rounding a rocky point that jutted out from the north, the men let the horses wander along the trail, while they turned off to force their way up a northern tributary.

The canyon was short, but narrow and brush-choked. At the head, the walls fell back, leaving a small open place the lower end of which was blocked by a huge rock that had split off the wall above. Over this grew a big cat-claw * bush, filling the canyon to the opposite wall. The men pushed their way through the prickly branches that hung over the water-puddled draw. A coyote that had been bent on the same errand as the men, turned at bay in the cave, the horses shied, and the coyote slipped past and was

---

* This western shrub is a barberry (*Berberis fremonti*), and is also called thimbleberry; the Utes call it *wee-ump*. In the spring, the yellow flowers grow in clusters and fill the canyons with an over-powering perfume. The fruit, a shell around a cluster of seeds, makes beautiful jelly. Birds feed on the berries to some extent, and coyotes pull clusters down and gorge, regurgitating seeds in ropy masses.

gone. Bob mused that this would be the same kind of trap for men in this close place, if a posse should come up the canyon. This very thing was to happen in the years to come, but not to him.

Leaving their saddle horses by the big rock, they stepped into the cool, cracklike cave where the water seeped from the sides and bottom. Scooping the sand from a depression in the narrow rock floor, they squatted on their bootheels and waited for water to gather and clear for a drink. Bob looked up at the narrow crack in the cave roof thirty feet above him, and wondered how many centuries of rainwater floods it had taken to cut through the roof of the cave—small streams, trickles really, judging from the narrowness of the cleft.

After drinking their fill and replenishing the water bag, the men wearily mounted again and made their way down the wash to the trail, turning left up the Roost Draw and overtaking the horses. A few more steers and some antelope spooked out of the big brush as they jingled past.

Bob soon discovered that the sand in the widening Roost Draw was far too thirsty to permit runoff no matter how much rain a thunderstorm dropped into the rising valley up which the outfit was kicking up dust. Side trails came down the shallow side washes (mostly from the south), merging with the main trail crossing the vast sand dunes and winding among the rounded sandstone buttes that rose stark from the blow-sand.

Low brush grew profusely among the dunes, the pungent herbage of the desert. Indian rice grass, which Bob called sand grass, grew stirrup high. This was the wonderful feed of the high deserts, heading twice a year in May and September, which had furnished breadstuff for the Indians. The hungry horses snatched at the heavy seedheads as the men hurried them along.

Evening activity of the small folk of the desert became evident after the punishing sun dropped low. Rabbits hopped among the stunted brush and little gray birds darted out of hidden nests. Once Bob heard the buzzing of a rattler, disturbed by the vibration of the ground, but it was getting late, and they didn't stop to kill it.

Almost sooner than he expected, they plodded over a sand dune and Cap turned the horses toward the cedars on the left. They caught the willing pack mule and hobbled the rest of the horses, then set up the simple camp. After their scanty supper, the two men settled down for low-voiced talk. Long before dark, they spread their blankets on flat places on the clean sand, and Bob lay down tiredly in the soft twilight.

Far to the south and west across the spread of the Roost Flats, Dead Man's Hill was etched against the afterglow. Bob let his gaze range along the cedar-feathered ridge east of it, where dusk was blurring the shallow buffalo-grass swales that swept up from the draw near him. The beautiful country purpled softly as hollows filled with shadow and night crept over the land. He could smell a faint breath of dust the hobbled horses had stirred on the hillside, and with it the crushed herbage together with a flower scent that he was to learn came from the night-blooming sand puffs.

As he dropped off to sleep, the boy could not know that in a few short years the Roost Flats would be dotted with cattle and horses of the 3B outfit, and that he would often be a welcome rider in their camp—not far from where he was camped on this first trip into Robbers Roost.

The next morning Cap turned back and Bob started the horses north across the open San Rafael Desert. He would cross the Green River at the mouth of the San Rafael River, and the Colorado near Moab, heading south and then east to Telluride.

Mr. and Mrs. Arthur Ekker, present owners of Robbers Roost, at the water troughs at Robbers Roost Spring as they look today. The original troughs are set against the bank around the turn and opposite the ledge in this picture.

—PHOTO COURTESY OF PARKER HAMILTON, FLAGSTAFF, ARIZONA

THE 3B OUTFIT
FEEDS THE WILD BUNCH

Like the sign, "This is a non-profit organization—but we didn't intend to be," the 3B outfit miscalculated—nor did they intend to be an outlaw hangout.

J. B. Buhr, a tailor from Denver, brought a herd of cattle and a band of good mares with a fine stallion named Major into the Roost in the early 1890's. He had suffered for years from asthma, and he and his two brothers had invested in the livestock, hoping a life in the open air would improve his health.

It might have done so, too, if Buhr had taken a more active interest in the business. He wouldn't ride the range himself, but depended entirely on a hired crew under a foreman.

His first foreman was Joe Bernard, under whose supervision the Roost Spring was put into troughs for the first time. Until then, livestock had watered in the puddles and pools in the draw. Bernard hired Dennis * to drive a

---
* Dennis left his name in the country briefly—the oldtimers called the Spur Fork of Horseshoe Canyon "Dennis Canyon," but since my family didn't know that, when we moved to Robbers Roost in 1909, we named it Spur Fork, and that is what it is called today.

wagon loaded with a camp outfit and some lumber out through the trackless wastes from Hanksville to the Roost.

He built three small troughs, and using the wagon over the primeval range—printing the first wheel tracks across the Roost Flats—he hauled small cedar posts cut around Buhr Pass and Blue John to fence in a little plot around the headbox of the spring on the sidehill. Later the plot was enlarged to take in one of the cottonwoods, and one of the troughs was removed. Some say the lumber in the trough was needed for a door in the cabin that Jack Cottrell built a few years later.

When the stallion Major died, Buhr bought another horse from a man by the name of Parker (no relation to Bob Parker) in Grass Valley. He called the horse Park, and the big bay horse with a star in his forehead and one white hind foot lived to leave the country with Buhr in 1900.

Bernard quit because the Roost was too far away from his home in the Sevier Valley and Buhr hired Jack Cottrell as foreman, moving the headquarters first to Hanksville, then to Granite at the foot of the Henry Mountains. Granite Wash ran a good stream of water, and he planned to make a real ranch there. But he never did any farming himself, and it is a cinch Jack Cottrell didn't intend to pitch hay.

Around the mountain from Granite, Fairview had been settled by a fellow named Tomlinson. The name for this ranch had been well chosen, since it afforded a broad view of Burr Desert, across to the Roost, and far away to the north to the Book Cliffs across the sandy San Rafael Desert. To the west the beautiful red canyons of Capitol Reef were backed by the hazy Thousand Lake Mountains. The ranch was set at the foot of Bull Mountain of the Henrys, which rose abruptly behind it.

With his wife, Lida Ellen, and three little boys, Tomlinson brought a sizable bunch of cows, and quite a string of good brood mares to Fairview. When he had raised enough colts (about thirty head) to make a drive to the mines of Colorado, he left for there, going by way of Green River. He wrote to his wife from Grand Junction, saying he was on his way to Montrose, and that is the last that was ever heard from him. Once a week for months, Mrs. Tomlinson rode in to Hanksville from Fairview in the hope there would be some word from him.

One day she happened to be in Hanksville when a man rode in on Hoppy, her husband's favorite saddle horse. She replevined the horse, but the fellow couldn't tell her anything except that he had bought the horse in Colorado.

The ranch at Fairview was too much of a responsibility for the lovely Lida Ellen. She wanted to live in town, or at least where there were a few neighbors. In her indecision about what to do, an incident occurred that settled the matter.

One morning Mirt, her oldest boy, started down to the corral under the hill to milk the cow. He was followed a little later by Bill, his three-year-old brother. Running back to see what Bill was setting up such a howl about, Mirt found a big bobcat holding him by the seat of the pants. Mrs. Tomlinson heard the commotion, ran out with a gun and killed the cat. But that settled it—she moved her family in to Hanksville.

Jack Cottrell was then foreman for Buhr at the Roost, with headquarters in Hanksville. From the first, he paid court to the lovely young widow with the sizable outfit and three little boys. As soon as it was settled beyond doubt that Tomlinson had met with foul play, Lida had him declared legally dead, and she and Cottrell were married.

Cottrell had been raised in Pennsylvania. He had joined a circus when he was in his teens and had been badly injured by an elephant, necessitating a silver plate in his skull. He was a big, dark-complexioned man, nice looking, with blue eyes, slightly curly dark brown hair and a prominent nose. Although he was fairly good natured, he was given to maniacal rages, with his old head injury giving him trouble from time to time. His sons tell of how he would sulk for days, then flare into violent fury.

He was, however, a fine hand with stock, took good care of his horses and cattle, and was a far better foreman for Buhr than Jack Moore, who took that job as soon as he came into the country.

The first cabin at Crow Seep, now the bunkhouse, was built by
the author's father.

—PHOTO COURTESY OF MILLIE BIDDLECOME, SALT LAKE CITY, UTAH

Robbers Roost troughs, with the author's father, Joe Biddlecome,
at right.

—PHOTO BY PEARL BAKER

During Cottrell's reign at the Roost, he moved his family there, building, with the help of Joe Sylvester, a cabin for them just above the Roost Spring. The chimney of the cabin is still standing, but many years later a sheepherder attempted to burn a rat's nest out of the corner of the cabin, and was all too successful.

The one room was built of cedar posts, stockade fashion. Posts from the scrubby cedar trees in the Roost area are short and crooked. It was easier to build a seven-foot high stockade than to lay the posts flat and splicing them together to build a wall took two or three times as long.* There was one small cloth-covered window in the east wall beside the door. The roof was constructed of small posts covered with cedar bark and a generous layer of red gypsum clay to more or less seal out the rain and snow.

Up on the ledge nearby, the ends of a rocky shelf were fenced in by short rock walls, making a corral for horses. Underneath, a blacksmith shop was set up, with a few simple tools, mostly horseshoeing equipment.

Here the Tomlinson-Cottrell family lived in the cabin and a tent, getting water from a little spring nearby, which is almost dried up today. Cottrell set a barrel in the ground under the spring to catch the meager ooze of clear, sweet water. On washdays, Mrs. Cottrell went by saddle horse to Silver Tip Spring, where Parker had found a drink a few years before.

Bill Tomlinson was about five or six at that time, and he says he remembers the cattle, mostly roan or spotted, stringing through the tall brush past the cabin into the Roost to water. The bulls walked with heads swinging low, murmuring a steady rumble of threats, stopping every few yards to swing up their heavy heads and bellow out a challenge far and wide. Pawing up a few hoof-fulls of red trail dust to throw over their shoulders to show how mean they were, and to drive off the flies that gathered in a cloud on the heavy shoulders and swollen necks of the big brutes, they would bellow again, their uproar rising to a chilling

---

* My father, Joe Biddlecome, found that out when he built the first cabin at the headquarters at Crow Seep. It is now the bunkhouse. That he was able to lay up a wall of any kind with the logs he had is a monument to his skill, but they stand just as sturdy and true as when he spliced them together over fifty years ago.

scream of defiance. They then would lower their heads, swing them from side to side as they plodded down the trail, cursing menacingly again. Sometimes they stopped to sharpen their wicked horns on the catclaw brush along the trail. These bushes retained a one-sided growth from such rough pruning for a good long time—I remember them distinctly forty years later.

On the trails leading in from Dead Man's Hill area, cattle plodded down the sand draws and over dunes, their tracks constantly erased in the sand, but the trails on the slickrock were cut in sometimes as much as six inches. The trails looked that way to Bob Parker, and they look that way today. Bill Tomlinson said they were the same when he was a child, and he thought the original trails had been cut by bison, a few ancient bones could still be found when he lived there. Indians had told him that the "big snow" had killed the buffalo—"Big snow, seven Utes deep."

But that was a long time before the little Tomlinson boys, mounted on mettlesome stick horses, played cops and robbers in the brush and over the rocks and ridges of the Roost Draw. They gave the universal game of the West an unusual twist—as they played it, the U.S. Marshal was always the one that got shot!

After a year or two at the Roost, Cottrell moved his family back to Hanksville, where they lived for several years. He seems to have quit the 3B about that time, probably to take care of his own outfit, and Jack Moore became foreman for Buhr.

Moore may have cut Cottrell out of the job; the two men were bitter enemies. They had several serious clashes before Cottrell finally picked up and left the country around the turn of the century.

During Jack Moore's foremanship for the 3B outfit, more and more outlaws drifted into the country and gathered at Robbers Roost. Some of them seemed to know where they were going, and all of them found a welcome at the camp Jack Moore set up above Roost Spring. These men came to be known as the Wild Bunch, and Jack Moore contributed his share to their fame.

JACK MOORE

The dream of vast cattle empire held by the Buhr brothers of Denver was doomed the day J. B. Buhr hired Jack Moore as foreman. Ten years later (1900), when J. B. found his asthma still with him, but not many of his horses and cattle, he gave up. Selling what cattle he could gather, he took the stallion Park, and a few mares, and with Mrs. Jack Moore (Jack had been killed by then) left the country. Word drifted back that they were killed in a railway crossing accident somewhere in Texas.

During the time the 3B cattle ranged the Roost, Jack Moore extended the hospitality of the outfit to the Wild Bunch. It is said he never hired a hand other than the kid, Neil Hanks; there were enough outlaws around all the time to make a crew. The Roost became the southern hide-out for the same men who used Hole-in-the-Wall and Browns' Hole, and here they bunched up ten or fifteen at a time during off seasons—although one group spent the winter at the mouth of White Canyon, across from Hite on the Colorado River.

Summer was outlaw time; winter horseback riding was too uncomfortable, and tracks lasted too long in snow and frozen mud. Horses didn't stay very fat, either, pawing grass out of two feet of wet or frozen snow.

In the 1880's, when the big cattle drives of the West were over, there was no place for the cowboys to land. Some of them settled down to work on ranches or with small outfits of their own. The more enterprising and restless, those whose eyes always had looked beyond the far ridge and whose ears were attuned to the night voices of the open spaces, wandered disconsolately between Texas and Mexico behind livestock not their own. When the Texas Rangers cleaned up down there, some of the boys faded north, and most of them landed in southern Colorado. Learning of the remoteness and good horse feed at the Roost, they came on over, many of them seeming to have known Moore elsewhere.

Jack Moore was one of the first of these; he had worn the sobriquet of Dee Jackson in southwestern Colorado. He crossed the Blues (Abajo Mountains), probably through the Bear's Ears, dropped down White Canyon, crossed the Colorado River at Dandy Crossing, and headed up Trachyte toward the Henry Mountains. He ran onto Neil Hanks, a Mormon boy from Hanksville (which his father had founded only a few years before), herding cattle for Sanford, a local rancher at the head of Granite Wash. Jack stopped to pass the time of day, got to talking, and finally rode into the cow camp to spend the night.

During the evening he learned about the gold-mining camp on the Henrys at Eagle City, and left the next morning to look it over. He decided to winter there, and go on his way when the weather broke the next spring. He was a good gambler, and he made a little stake off the miners during the winter. There, too, he met Grimes and Ricker, a friendship that was to bear fruit later. And somehow he caught the eye of J. B. Buhr.

Jack was a striking-looking cowboy, six feet three inches tall, extremely thin, with black curly hair, a black moustache, and swarthy skin. He was about thirty-five, quick and active, well able to take care of himself among his rough companions. His black eyes snapped, he was witty and fond of a joke, roaring with honest appreciation of his own humor. He carried a pearl-handled sixshooter, a .44 that shot the same ammunition as his .44 saddle rifle. He smoked a pipe, packing it with cut-up plug chewing tobacco. He wore woolen pants and shirt, the rough riding clothes of the times, topped by a big black hat. In that era, when horses were of such importance and everyone was a good horseman, Jack was really outstanding, handling his mount with skill and conducting himself on the range with fine judgment.

The other riders always knew Jack as far as they could see him. He sat his horse with his head down and his big hat pulled low to shade his eyes as he scanned the ground for tracks. He claimed he could follow a cow's tracks for a hundred yards and tell what color she was, and while that was his idea of a joke, his tracking ability was simply un-canny; he was known for it almost as much as for his droll humor.

Jack would lift his hat, run his fingers through his crisp, curly hair and say, "Tell you, boys, they sure did like me in Texas. A bunch of ranchers followed me clean across the state to try to get me back—and they'd have done it, too, if Minnie hadn't been faster than anything they rode!" And he would guffaw at his sally.

Minnie was the little race mare, black, with one white hind foot, that he had ridden into the country. Mares were almost never ridden in the West, and one had to be as out-standing as Minnie or Babe, the bay mare used in the Castle Gate holdup, to be considered at all. Minnie never did have a colt, and was usually in Jack's string.

He also rode a big, black 〤 (TV) * horse he called Turk. Turk would buck every time he had a week's rest, and Jack was about the only hand who could top him out.

The cabin above the Roost Spring didn't suit Moore—it was too far from horse feed—so he moved camp three miles east to Dugout (as it came to be called) in Buhr

---

* 〤 was the Buhr brothers' horse brand. It was cusomary to use a different iron for horses, and the Buhrs used 3B for cattle and 〤 for horses. It was pronounced TV.

Pass, at the head of the Roost Draw. There, close to where
Bob Parker had camped, he built a part-dugout part-shed
to live in. Later he brought in a tent to shelter the in-
creased crew from snow and storm.

Neil Hanks, the Mormon boy, who had been almost the
first native Jack had met when he entered the area, used
to stay at the Roost a good deal. His family was poor, and
the outfit paid him well to jingle (bring in) the horses,
cook, and do other chores. Forty years later he liked to tell
about Jack coming to the door of the dugout and saying,
"Get up, Kid, and cook these boys some supper," when a
new bunch drifted in between dark and daylight.

Neil must have been a little mixed up in his own mind
about which riders were outlaws and which were not; who
was "bad" and who was "good" among the men he knew.
He asked Jack one time to straighten him out on it, and
Jack answered typically:

"Well, I'll tell you, Kid, outlaws are just fellows, some
of them good and some of them no-good. But there's one
thing about them," eyeing the blond Mormon boy, who
had several married sisters and brothers, "they are usually
better looking than in-laws, and a hell of a sight easier to
live with."

Jack started to dig a well at Dugout, but remarked that
from the looks of things, it was about as far to water in
that direction as it was down the trail to the Roost—but
the going was harder. Water for camp was carried in kegs
and waterbags from the little sweet spring above the
Roost, the one later called Silver Tip, and once a day the
horses were driven to the Roost to water.

Today it is simply beyond belief how much time these
men spent on just routine care of their horses. Of course,
their mounts were vital; a man without a horse was almost helpless in that thinly settled country. But never
think that men idled away their time. They spent hard,
tedious hours every day breaking and training saddle
horses, and a good share of the remaining time was spent
in keeping the animals on the best feed, or taking them
long distances to water.

The 3B outfit camped at Buhr Pass for upward of ten

years. It was there that Headlight, the old brown horse
with the big round star in his forehead, kicked the little
dog Sunday and broke his leg. Sunday belonged to Neil,
since these men traveled too far and fast for the luxury of
pets. They liked Sunday, and it didn't endear Headlight
to them for him to commit such an offense. Neil splinted
the leg and carried the puppy in a nosebag on his saddle
until the leg healed. Sunday was still around in 1897, five
or six years later, following the boys from the horse change
at Mexican Bend on the return from the Castle Gate
holdup.

Jack's sense of humor was sometimes a little crude, and
not always enjoyed by everyone. One time he went into
Farrers' Store in Green River to buy some pants. Being so
tall, he said he would like to try them on for fit. Matt Riley,
the clerk, gave them to him, and took him to a back room
to change. Jack put the pants on, then called for different
sizes and kinds until he had donned six pairs. He then came
out front, paid for the outermost pair and walked stiffly
out. Riley was well aware that he had not collected the full
bill, but such was Jack's reputation as a gunman that the
transaction went uncontested. Jack thought it the best
joke of the season and often boasted about it. But Riley's
sense of humor was dim.

Jack was as tough as he acted. One time, while roping
cattle at the Roost, he tied onto a big, fat cow, and she
jerked his horse down. After Jack got untangled from the
mixup, he found his shoulder had been pulled out of place.
This was a common range injury, and the method used
to re-set a dislocated shoulder was to roll up a coat tightly,
place it under the armpit, and have someone give the arm
a sharp jerk over it. Usually the joint snapped right back
into place, and aside from being lame for a few days no
further treatment was considered necessary.

This didn't work with Jack. He had torn some ligaments
loose, and the efforts to re-set the shoulder only made mat-
ters worse. In a week or ten days he went into Grand
Junction to see a doctor, who told people later that he had
never seen such an injury: the arm was pulled almost
loose from its socket. Jack had never complained, but the

doctor seemed to think it must have been agonizingly painful.

After Moore had been foreman for Buhr for a while, he sent for his wife, Nora. Her brother, Monte Butler, brought her and his own wife in through Green River, across the San Rafael Desert, past Hanksville to the ranch at Granite, at the foot of the Henry Mountains.

The Butlers stayed around a year or two, giving their name to several washes and other landmarks, then returned to Colorado, but Mrs. Moore stayed several years at Granite, where she nursed Buhr, whose asthma was getting worse all the time.

She made a home for the cowboys of the 3B (the Wild Bunch). She was cultured and pleasant, had good taste, and softened the harsh cabin with pictures, sofa pillows, and other luxuries. She wouldn't let the boys smoke or swear in the house, but they didn't seem to resent it. They ate their meals in the kitchen and sat in the parlor to read and visit.

Buhr, having been a tailor in Denver before his brothers and he bought the 3B outfit, made the two women fancy riding costumes. These must have been veritable works of art, all the oldtimers can remember how beautiful they were.

Jack spent most of his time at the Roost, but went to Granite often, traveling either the Angel Trail, or going around by Hanksville. He also had cattle interests of his own around the Henry Mountains.

There were thousands of cattle in those days, the range was wonderful, and cattle-raising was the leading industry. Jack couldn't bear to see the range get overstocked seemingly, and what "Lutheran-fed" beef he couldn't eat or feed to the Wild Bunch, he just relocated. Mormons have a legend that their first alfalfa seed came from Switzerland, and they called it *lucerne* for that reason, but Jack wouldn't settle for that pronunciation. During some of the worst winter weather owners would take in their weak stock and feed them hay (lucerne hay, that is), so Jack called any cow fed hay "Lutheran-fed," which gradually came to mean to him and his brother-rustlers any cow belonging to the local ranchers.

He gathered and shifted these herds around constantly in small bunches—to the mines in Colorado and the shipping points on the railroad at Cisco, Green River and Woodside. This was usually done in the winter time when the owners were snugly at home, and the loss was not discovered until spring. All cattle ran on the open range, and there were no general roundups, so no man knew exactly how many cattle he had, nor could he lay his hands on all of them at any given time. Finally Jack grew ambitious and, with the help of Grimes and Ricker, raided Thompson, Starr, Sanford and others, and drove the herd to Telluride, Colorado. (This is covered in Chapter 10.)

Returning to the 3B outfit, Jack started to gather the Buhr cattle for shipment, as J. B. was selling and leaving the country. This was in 1898.

While riding the outside ranges, Jack and another fellow found a big unbranded calf on the San Rafael Desert. The calf was following a cow carrying Hebe Wilson's brand, but according to their lights this didn't necessarily make the calf Hebe's if they got it first.

They roped the calf and began leading it away. It was fat, strong and unruly, and they had their hands full. The cow (which they would haze back, shoot or handle as the occasion warranted when they got around to her) was following the calf, bawling. Ben Gibbons and Jack Cottrell rode up, and this was exactly what Cottrell had been hoping for. He and Ben lit a shuck for town, swore out a complaint and had Jack Moore arrested. But Buhr and little Black Pete Jensen went his bond for $1,000, each putting up $500.

Jack was to stand trial at Castle Dale, but he didn't show up. He sent word for Pete to meet him at Temple Mountain and get his bond money. Jack rode from the Roost to keep the appointment, gave Pete the $500 and started back to the Roost, where his being outside the law was no disadvantage.

He watered his horse at Straight Wash, which turned out to be a mistake. Sometimes the Straight Wash water seemed to be poisonous and would kill a horse either immediately or make it so sick the rider was everything but

J. B. Buhr built the first two rooms of the cabin at Granite. The one on the farther end was added later. The rock cellar on the right was built by Frank Webber. The door on the end had the knob shot off by a posse that believed Jack Moore was in the cabin and would not come out.

—PHOTO BY PEARL BAKER

afoot. Jack made for San Rafael when his horse began failing, and by taking his time and coaxing the animal along made it to Chris Halverson's ranch. All he could borrow was an old sorrel horse, but he decided it would carry him to the Roost.

Losing his horse had made him horse-conscious, and he got to thinking he'd better get the saddle horses from the ranch, too, so he changed his mind and headed for Granite. He skirted the town of Hanksville, not intending to call in, but some of the town youngsters saw him and ran to tell Sheriff Rufe Stoddard that Jack was in the vicinity, alone.

Moore went on to Granite. He and Aikens were corralling some horses that he planned to take back to the Roost when Stoddard and Cottrell rode up the draw. The outlaws (although no one considered Aikens an outlaw—just a damn good fellow who would take a hand in anything that was going on) left the horses and took off up the draw, rounding a point, and none too soon, either! They jumped off their horses, got their guns and climbed up on the little ridge with the intention of moving the law back out of range.

"Shoot that sonofabitch on the sorrel horse," Jack yelled to Aikens for the benefit of the lawmen. "I want that horse." But they didn't shoot to kill anyone. The sorrel horse, Nubbins, belonged to Jean Sanford and was famous for speed and endurance.

The officers dropped back in a side wash where Aikens kept them entertained, while Jack, still on the Halverson horse, changed his mind and thought he had better make for the Roost and sanctuary. Dropping down the draw, he kept out of sight as much as possible and got past Stoddard and Cottrell.

As soon as he was safely by, Aikens found other things to do, and the lawmen started up the draw. As soon as they cut Jack's trail, they knew what had happened. Putting spurs to their mounts, they gave chase, flushing him out in a mile or so. The old sorrel horse was slow and unwilling, but Jack was persuasive and made Beaver Box ahead of the officers, just at dusk. He raced down the canyon and across the Dirty Devil River, only jumps ahead of them. There he jerked off his saddle and turned the old horse loose, starting it back up the canyon so Stoddard and Cottrell wouldn't pot it in their enthusiasm.

The two-man posse followed across the river, but Jack stood them off from behind a big rock until dark. During the run down Beaver Box his gun, shoved in the waistband of his pants, had fallen out, but he was too pressed to go back for it. He armed himself with a burnt stub out of a bunch of fire-killed willows and, thrusting this black stick from behind the rock, jeered, "I only got a few bullets, so I'm waiting for you to come closer. Come on, boys."

They smoked him up some, but didn't dare call his bluff, although they had picked up his gun and were reasonably sure he was unarmed. After dark he easily gave them the slip, walking back up the river where he was lucky enough to find a sheep camp. He borrowed a horse and, sending word by the sheepherder to Chris Halverson that he had lost the horse and that if it didn't show up he would make it good, he picked up his saddle and headed for the Roost. He sent the sheepherder's horse right back, but Chris was several months getting the old sorrel home again.

The 3B cattle were pretty much gathered into their home range at the Roost, and had been sold by Buhr. Jack, with the help of Silver Tip, Blue John and Indian Ed Newcomb, finished throwing them together and trailed them across the desert for delivery at Green River, Utah. This was the last bunch to be sold and there were only some two hundred head.

While holding the herd at San Rafael for a day or two to rest and fill up, Jack learned from a passing cowboy that there was a bench warrant out for him for the Hebe Wilson calf affair. He and Indian Ed stayed on San Rafael while the other two took the cattle in and delivered them.

Around the campfire the night the two returned from Green River, Moore, Silver Tip, Blue John and Indian Ed decided to seek new country. All the Buhr cattle—and most of the stock belonging to other ranchers—were gone, and these four had accounted for a good share of their disappearance. There was no point in going back to the Roost, so they made a trip to Wyoming to pick up a few horses for the Colorado trade.

Near Baggs they rounded up a sizable herd belonging to a rancher named Spicer, who took an exceedingly limited view of losing his horses out of the home fields and followed them hotly. Several shots had been exchanged, but the boys were making their getaway in good shape without losing a horse, when Spicer drew in too close.

"You fellows go on, and I'll go up on this knoll and give him a farewell shot," Jack yelled.

From the top of the knoll, he did shoot once but left himself wide open, and Spicer was playing for keeps. He pulled down "from a mile away," according to Neil Hanks who heard the story from the boys when they returned, "and drilled Jack dead center with a 30-30 slug.

"The boys saw that Jack was hit, and Ed and Silver Tip went on with the horses, while Blue John went back to Jack. He took him to Mid Nichol's saloon, and Mid found them a place to stay. Jack lingered a few days, but he was shot through the middle and couldn't make it. Mid paid his funeral expenses, sent a bill to Mrs. Jack Moore at Hanksville, and she sent him a check for it."

In 1899 Mrs. Moore and Buhr hired a crew to gather the horses at the Roost and prepared to leave the country. She herded the horses, and Buhr brought the camp outfit in a buggy. They drove the horses up Huntington Canyon, but must have changed their minds and veered off toward Texas, as word drifted back some months later they had been killed in a railroad crossing accident there.

The next winter (1900), with the fight at the Roost (Chapter XI), the era of the Wild Bunch at the Roost closed. Most of the boys had drifted out of the country, and the Wild Bunch was plying its nefarious trade elsewhere. However there was one man who didn't forget them, since he had tried for years to be accepted into their ranks. This was Gunplay Maxwell, who lived about as futile an outlaw existence as it would be possible to imagine.

GUNPLAY (C. L.) MAXWELL

The Wild Bunch didn't look upon Gunplay Maxwell as one of them, although he associated with them occasionally and considered himself one of their number. His efforts to prove to the boys that he was tough enough to join their forces somehow never came out exactly as he had planned. Whether he was a fumbler, or just had the worst luck in the world, his outlaw forays turned out to be farces.

Long after Butch Cassidy and his boys were gone from the country, Gunplay was still trying to prove his toughness. Once while traveling from Green River toward the Henry Mountains in a buckboard loaded (both Gunplay and the buckboard) with bad whiskey, he seized an opportunity to prove himself. Ebb Gillies was taking a load of hay to Green River to sell and he met Gunplay on top of one of the blue clay hills just out of town. With Ebb was Joe Nougier, and Gunplay ordered the two boys down off the load to dance while he played Colt's music for them. After about the second shot at their heels, Slick Nickerson, who had been catching up on his sleep for the trip to town,

46

peered over the edge of the hay to see what was taking place. Sizing up the situation, he slid off the far side and walked stealthily around to the back of the buggy. Before Gunplay realized he was no longer in control of the situation, Slick reached over the seat of the buckboard and seized the gun. He then proceeded to pistol whip Maxwell with his own gun—a final insult!—and sent him off down the road wiser, and cold sober.

Gunplay had drifted into the country by rail to Green River in the early '90s, where he outfitted himself and went western. That fall he threw in with another saddle bum named Porter, pretty much the same kind of fellow, although people liked Porter better. Together they took a contract to furnish beef to the gold camp killing the wild cedar cattle and butchering them on the range.

There were numerous wild cattle along the breaks of the mountains—big cows and bulls that had, for the most part, never been rounded up and branded. The ones that did carry an iron were either so old that their owners had moved out of the country, or so wild they couldn't be forced out of the timber, and the only way to gather them was with a 30-30 rifle. The two men were, therefore, accepted by the local ranchers—until they expanded their activities to include gentle stock.

Not much outlay was required for this project. Their camp outfit was simple, including a few staple groceries and a meager bed roll which they loaded onto an old white packhorse they called Bedwagon. Cartridges were about their only expense, until Maxwell lost his rifle making a run through the timber after a wild cow and had to buy another.

This life just suited Maxwell, he was at last in the Wild West, and doing the things that would make him an outlaw. He could ride, he could shoot—all he needed was for the boys to let him join up.

For some reason the two fellows didn't get into trouble over the beef. So many people were "working on" the cattle in that area that a few head were not even missed. Sometimes they were alone for a spell and sometimes the Tomlinson boys rode with them, or anyone else joined in who enjoyed a run through the timber after the wily "slow elk."

Gunplay got tired of getting rich slowly, especially since he usually lost the gains at poker before he could get out of the gold-mining camp after a delivery of beef. He wandered to Price, where he felt the stirrings of interest in the law-enforcement branch of the West. He hadn't done so well as an outlaw, so he changed tactics: If he couldn't join 'em, he'd fight 'em.

According to the County (Carbon) Court Minute Book No. 1, June, 1894 to December, 1900, at a meeting of the commissioners in April, 1897, just a few days before the Castle Gate holdup, Sheriff Donant of Price presented the name of C. L. Maxwell for deputy sheriff to the board for confirmation. There was a great deal of argument, and the matter was tabled until the next meeting. At that same meeting Commissioner Edgar Thayne entered a motion that "a reward of $250 be offered for the capture and evidence to convict Jos. Walker on charge of Grand Larceny, or the attempt to commit murder on the person of Sheriff Tuttle." (See Chapter 7.)

Before the meeting was over, Donant had presented a bill for $35 to C. L. Maxwell, which was disallowed. However, that doesn't mean too much—more claims were disallowed at that five-day meeting than were ordered paid. Donant brought up the matter of confirming Maxwell for deputy at one of the last meetings, and the "County Attorney, J. W. Warf presented opinions to Board which was (sic) read and filed." The contents were not set forth. (Remember this was just before the Castle Gate holdup, and either the law officers had been warned, or considered it was time for the Wild Bunch to strike again.)

Quoting from the minutes again, J. L. Smith, special officer of the Pleasant Valley Coal Company, presented to the board the following resolution:

> Whereas: There has been and now is within the confines of Carbon County a band of desperados who have at sundry times and places committed offences and openly violated the laws of Carbon, State; and

Whereas: No effort has been made by the sheriff to capture said lawless band and to put an end to such lawlessness;

Whereas: It has been reported to the members of the board of County Commissioners by reputable citizens of this county that the Sheriff of this county, Gus Donant, has refused and wilfully neglected to perform the duties of his office as sheriff to the detriment of the *best citizens and taxpayers*, and to the disgrace of the county; and

Whereas: the petition of Jas. L. Smith, Special Officer of the Pleasant Valley Coal Company recites and sets forth in more tangible form the reports which have from time to time been reported to the members of the Board of County Commissioners;

Now, therefore, be it resolved that the said sheriff of Carbon, Gus Donant, be and is hereby requested to hand in his resignation as sheriff of Carbon County forthwith to the end that a citizen may be appointed who will perform the duties of this office without fear or favor, that the county may regain her good name and become once more a desirable place for peaceable citizens to locate and settle, in which capital may be invested with safety.

And be it further resolved: That if the said sheriff refuses to resign, the County Attorney is hereby instructed to institute proceedings against him on the charges set forth in the petition of Jas. L. Smith, Special Officer of the Pleasant Valley Coal Company or any other charges which he may be able to find evidence to sustain, also ordered that the Clerk be instructed to notify the sheriff of the above action.

Page 163—Resignation of Sheriff Gus Donant read and accepted.

Page 164—It was ordered by the Board that C. W. Allred be appointed Sheriff of Carbon County. . . . Hood and Thayne voted affirmatively, Tidwell voted negative.

Judging from these meager notes, those county commissioner meetings must have been something to attend. Every issue was fought to a bitter finish, and there were no yes-men on the board.

Men who lived through this period, especially stockmen, do not paint exactly the same picture. Joe Walker was making life so miserable for the Whitmores that they were demanding that something be done; presenting Gus Donant as either a coward or an incompetent is not a fair picture. Local opinion favored Joe, and since he was not bothering anyone else, it was generally believed he was justified. While Donant wasn't straining anything to make a capture, the written record is not without bias. Money (Whitmore's) talked, and got itself on the record.

When Maxwell was repudiated as a deputy, he decided to follow the Wild Bunch's example once more, and chose to stage a bank robbery to gain their attention. He threw in with Porter again and, about a year after the Castle Gate holdup by Butch Cassidy and Elzy Lay, aided by Joe Walker, which occurred shortly after the above County Commissioners' hassle, he and Porter held up the Springville Bank at Springville, Utah.

Granted he had some bad luck, but the strategy might have been improved with a little more careful planning. It is hard to imagine why he tackled the job in a buckboard. Did he underestimate the danger? Was he establishing a new technique? What possible reason could he have had for using so unwieldy a getaway vehicle?

Springville lies against the Wasatch Range, at the mouth of Hobble Creek Canyon, up which a horseman could make his way and get out of sight quickly. From there he could go over the mountain either to the Uintah Basin country, to Salt Lake City, or north to Wyoming. Within hours he could be far away, with his trail hard to pick up—on horseback, that is.

Gunplay chose Saturday morning as the proper time and, entering the bank together with Porter, presented an order for $200 to the bookkeeper. The cashier had just gone out, and the bookkeeper said that they would have to wait until he returned and he went on with other work.

This was a fine way to treat a bank robber! Maxwell drew his gun and said, "Look here, young man!"

The bookkeeper turned back and, looking right down a gun barrel, raised his hands. Porter remained at the teller's window, keeping him covered while Gunplay went into the teller's cage and started to grab all the money in sight piling it into a handkerchief. While he was fumbling around, he dropped a stack of twenty-dollar gold pieces, making a terrible clatter. As he reached over to pick them up, Porter took his attention off the bank clerk to see what the racket was, and the clerk lowered his right hand quickly and pressed an alarm button. The alarm was connected with Mr. Reynold's hardware store across the street.

Mr. Reynold was busy with a customer, but he looked up at the short ring of the alarm. It was not repeated, and he remarked that they could be a little more careful over there. He walked to the front of the store and looked across the street. There didn't seem to be any excitement at the bank. The only living thing he could see on that side of the street was a horse hitched to a buggy. The lumber wagon, belonging to his customer, was on the hardware side of the street and up a few feet. All looked serene. Still, Mr. Reynold was a careful man, so he turned to the phone.

The ringing of the phone scared Gunplay nearly out of his wits. He clutched the corners of the handkerchief and backed out with Porter, who always followed Gunplay's lead without any protest. They got into the buggy and drove south, but as they got to the corner, all hell broke loose up the street.

When the phone wasn't answered, Reynold grabbed up a couple of Winchesters, rushed out on the street and, tossing one into the lumber wagon that was just ready to leave, got off a shot at the robbers as they turned the corner. This woke the town, and when Reynold went tearing after the buggy hell-for-leather in the lumber wagon, yelling "Bank robbers!" every man in town, who could, jumped on a saddle horse and gave chase. Springville was ordinarily a sleepy little farming village, and not in years had there been this much excitement.

At the edge of town the two outlaws met a man riding a fine saddle horse, and Gunplay drew his gun and ordered the man to dismount. Throwing a handful of coins, which later counted out to $46, down in front of the fellow, Gunplay mounted and rode away, leaving Porter still whipping up the buggy horse.

Mr. Reynold came on the scene in time to fire a couple of shots at the fleeing rider, but he neglected to stop the lumber wagon first, and the jolting caused his shots to go wild. The posse overtook the lumber wagon, their horses on a dead run. Gunplay and Porter looked back and, seeing what was coming, quit both the buggy and the horse and on foot took to the brush in the mouth of Hobble Creek Canyon.

The brush grew close together and rank as a jungle in the canyon, with a mat of leaves and twigs on the ground beneath. A few trails wound under the branches, and the two dived into one of these, thinking the brush extended up the canyon, unbroken. But the copse was small, and the posse soon surrounded it.

Joseph W. Allen, one of the ranchers, proposed that they form a line and march through the brush. This was a good idea, but the marching had to be done on hands and knees under the spreading branches. The march had not proceeded far when Gunplay's hiding place, under some leaves and branches, was overhauled and Gunplay taken into custody.

Porter, being somewhat more energetic than Gunplay, had made it farther into the brush. When he saw what was going on, he pulled his gun and started firing at the posse. His first bullet struck J. W. Allen just above the knee, knocking him over. Allen raised up on his elbow, took deliberate aim and shot Porter through the head, killing him instantly.

The posse took the outlaws back to town, where Gunplay told who he was, but for some reason never would tell who Porter was. He made no secret of Porter's identity when he returned to his old haunts, but he wouldn't tell the officers at the time of his arrest.

Gunplay had $2,083.50 on his person, about $300 was picked up in the brush, leaving $600 unaccounted for. Maxwell was taken to Provo for safekeeping and lodged in the pokey to await trail.

The newspaper at Price made a big thing of this. Maxwell was well but not favorably known there, and news was scarce in the middle of the summer. The fact was played up that Gunplay's wife wrote him from Eddyville, Massachusetts, saying she would stand by him. In the words of the *News Advocate:*

> . . . letter from his daughter. The little tot cannot write, but prints the letters. She says, "Dear Papa—I would like to see you; I do not forget you, Papa, and I love you. You are a good papa. Goodbye. From your daughter Merl." There were cross signs and the like representing kisses.

After serving a year or two in the state penitentiary, Gunplay came back into the Robbers Roost area. Since he had reflected very little glory on outlawry in general, he decided to start over as a total stranger to the country. It didn't work. Almost the first person he saw was Bill Tomlinson. Bill could remember plainly when Gunplay had lost his rifle while chasing a wild cow on the Henry Mountains during his beef-killing career. Gunplay argued, but finally had to admit his identity after Bill reminded him of the gun incident.

He stayed in the country prospecting and just fooling around for a year or two. In the early 1900s his wife (not the one in Massachusetts, she doesn't appear again) joined him with her grown son, Chauncy Humes. Chauncy was so extraordinarily tough he was wont to remark he "had a quart of blood for breakfast." Neilus Ekker, a native of Hanksville, hauled the trio and their supplies out to the placer claims at the head of North Wash, where they placer-mined for a season or two.

Around 1910, several years after the Wild Bunch had left the country, Maxwell and Shoot-'Em-Up-Bill Hatfield got into a hassle over some gilsonite claims in Sinbad. But Maxwell's feet wouldn't hold him in one spot long enough for them to get to shooting at each other, so a chance to eliminate two thorns in the side of society was muffed.

However, Maxwell was bound to get it, and get it he did —in Price, in a drunken brawl, when a guard at the Castle Gate Mine killed him. He was not mourned by many, and certainly by no member of the Wild Bunch, who never at any time claimed any affiliation with him or allowed him to associate with them. But since he considered himself a real wild and woolly bad man and was a contemporary of the Wild Bunch, if not a member save in his own estimation, his story points up what is not an acceptable outlaw.

Another man whose association with the Wild Bunch was more his idea than theirs, although a man of considerably higher caliber than Gunplay, was Matt Warner. He had ridden with the boys, and furnished them sanctuary at his horse ranch on Diamond Mountain near Browns Park, but except for his exploits with the McCartys, didn't engage in too much activity with the Wild Bunch in their forays. From his own accounts, he never was actually in Robbers Roost itself—but his story is nonetheless pertinent.

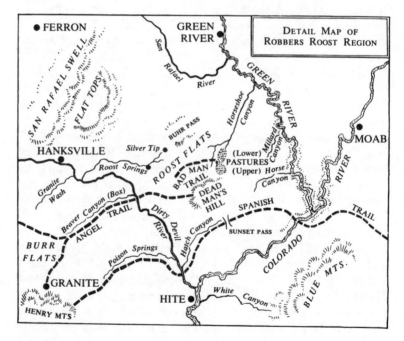

MATT WARNER

Matt Warner was born Willard Erastus Christianson at Ephraim in 1864, the son of a Swedish father and a German mother. The family was good stock, pioneer-poor as were most of the early families of central Utah. When Matt was small, they moved to Levan and lived there until he left home.

Levan was a little Mormon town, where most of the cultural and recreational activities were sponsored by the Church of Jesus Christ of Latter Day Saints, commonly called the LDS Church. Matt attended Sunday School, Mutual (the young people's organization, which sponsored all social activities for both boys and girls), and other affairs of the town. He followed the pattern of his generation, neither better nor worse than his contemporaries.

Being perfectly normal, when he was about fifteen he discovered girls—Alice Sabey, to be exact. Alice was pretty and she was popular, but Matt felt equal to the competition.

Andrew Hendrickson also preferred Alice, making bad blood between the boys, which erupted into fisticuffs one time on their way home from a dance where Matt had warned Andrew to leave Alice strictly alone. Andrew insisted that the best man win, and they went at it.

During the heat of the fight, Matt tore a picket off a fence by which they were scuffling and hit Andrew over the head with it. Andrew went down like a poll-axed steer, and Matt, unable to get any response to his frantic efforts at resuscitation, raced home. He wakened his parents and told them what had happened, then saddled his horse, and left the country.

Many years later, when I knew Matt, he had retained his vivid imagination and flavorful personality; life tasted just a little spicier on his tongue than on that of most of us. Therefore I can believe that when he left home at fifteen, and started over the mountain through the Strawberry country into the Uintah Basin, Jim Bridger had nothing on Matt. His stories of riding alertly through the woods, hiding his camps, avoiding Indian and white man alike (the latter being all U.S. marshals to him) made good telling in the years to come. It was true enough, indeed, but not everyone would have seen it and enjoyed it as much as Matt did.

He kept going across the Uintah Basin until he came to the extreme northeast corner of Utah, where he rode in to the ranch of Jim Warren on Diamond Mountain. Warren had a fine cattle outfit, and Matt learned a great deal about the stock business in the next two or three years. It became his ambition to own a horse ranch at Diamond Mountain, a dream he tried twice in the years to come to bring to a reality.

Some five or six years later, while working around at different jobs to get a stake for the horse ranch, Matt tried ferry-boating on the Green River at Ouray. One of his customers was an old childhood friend, who informed him that Andrew had recovered from the fence-picket blow and that Matt could go home any time he wanted to. But Diamond Mountain held him.

After this friend returned to Levan, Matt's thirteen-year-old nephew, Lew McCarty, Tom McCarty's oldest boy, came to stay with him. Matt could use a hand, and was glad to see the lad. He had started buying and trading for horses for his ranch at Diamond Mountain, and he needed a herd boy who wouldn't cost him much for wages.

Cattle and horse stealing were the order of the day in this area, remote from law enforcement, but if he was engaged in these activities, he didn't get into trouble. His ranch was isolated, however, and those men who rode dim trails stopped in. It's a cinch he knew the members of the Wild Bunch as soon as anybody did because they would always stop at outlying ranches.

Before he got really well established, the McCartys moved from central Utah to the La Sal Mountains in the southeastern part of the state. They sent for Lew to come home and, knowing Matt had a string of good horses, painted the advantages of that country for a horse ranch in glowing colors.

Matt took his horses to their ranch and went on down into New Mexico, just looking around. There he fell in with another saddle bum and they held up a trading post. Matt discovered it was easier to make money that way than any other he had found, and dropped in on the McCarty's at La Sal with his advanced ideas.

One of Matt's horses that the McCartys were taking care of for him was the race mare, Betty. He and Tom McCarty set out to spend the summer racing Betty all over the western slope of the Rockies. The Colorado mines at Telluride, Rico and other places were running full blast; there was plenty of money and the miners weren't too choosy how they spent it. Horse racing was a favorite sport, and each section of the country stood behind its favorite against all comers. Horse racing was then, as always, a lucrative business—with a good horse.

Betty was all of that: at the race in Telluride, it was almost a steal, she won so easily and so much. It was most natural that Matt should meet Butch Cassidy (at that time, Robert Parker). Matt won Butch's whole outfit on the race, then gave it back to him, and invited him to throw in with them in their racing ventures.

That just suited Butch. He may even have known Matt before, as it is said he made a trip to Wyoming and was around Hole-in-the-Wall for a time, returning to the mine at Telluride only about a year before.

He had gone back to packing ore down the mountain on burros, but he was heartily sick of hoisting heavy packs onto these little beasts of burden, then hazing them down to the mill. He was homesick for the open range and the outdoors.

The three traveled with Betty and their other horses, cleaning up around the country for a while. They took races from Gypsy Queen at Durango, Colorado, from the Cavanaugh stud at Mancos, and White Face, a one-eyed Indian pony, at McElmo Gulch.

The Indians bet all the money they had, then bet White Face, himself; but when Matt took the horse, the Indians changed their minds. The next morning a group of bucks came up to the cabin on McElmo Creek where Matt, Tom McCarty and Butch were staying. They called the white men out of the house and demanded their horse back. In the ensuing argument, when all hands were going at it hot and heavy, Tom lost his head and shot one of the Indians. They fled, taking the dead man with them.

The boys started saddling their horses to vacate before the redmen returned with reinforcements. Holding a brief council of war, they discussed how to get a stake in the quickest time. In spite of their race winnings, they were not too flush. They had lived pretty high, losing in gambling halls what they won at the race track.

Tom wished there was a bank handy. He couldn't think of a quicker way to make a pile of money. Butch spoke up, suggesting the Telluride Bank, then briefed them on the routine of the personnel. They could ride in, he said, hold up the bank and ride out again, before the townsmen were aware there was something wrong, if they did it at the right time of day. This sounded good, and they rode off, picking up Bert Madden on the way to wrangle horses.

After a successful robbery, they split up, landing in Wyoming that fall, working in different sections. Butch stopped in Rock Springs (where he earned the name "Butch") while Tom and Matt drifted over to Star Valley, on the border of Utah and Wyoming. Late fall snows caught them there and closed the mountain passes until the spring thaw. When they saw they would be holed up for a few months, they took the attitude that if they couldn't get out, the law officers couldn't get in, and they might as well enjoy themselves.

There were several ranches in the valley, and the two good-looking young cowboys batching in an abandoned log cabin settled right into the social pattern. Not since he had left home at Levan had Matt been the member of a small, close-knit community, and he enjoyed it.

They hadn't been there long when they discovered that some of the families, unable to go out for food and lacking the money to get it even if they had been able to leave, were starving. There was a small store in the valley, but the storekeeper wouldn't extend credit. Finally Matt and Tom, seeing their friends in want, laid down the law to the storekeeper and forced him to give the people food for half price, which they paid for with some of their robbery money. This put them in the social swim in a big way, and Matt met a girl, Rose Morgan. He had never planned to succumb to a girl's charms, but with Rose it was different.

A few of the Wild Bunch formed alliances with women, some of them of considerable validity and duration. Etta Place went to South America with Harry Longabaugh, the Sundance Kid, and Lay was married for a time to Maude Davis of Vernal. But this was much later than Matt's visit to Star Valley.

He chafed at the late spring, waiting for the snow to melt enough so he could take Rose to Montpelier. He and Tom knew the sheriff was very alert and laying for them, but it was the closest place Matt could find a preacher.

Finally the day came, and Matt and Rose, with Tom and Sary Lemberg, who had similar ideas, drove boldly over the mountain. The move was so open that no one noticed them at Montpelier as they drove into town and were married in the court house.*

The sheriff was out of town, he had gone to Star Valley by another road to capture Tom and Matt. When he re-

---

* Tom had been married to Matt's sister, and they had two boys, but she had died.

Trails carved into the rocks by animal hooves south of Robbers Roost Spring, with Arthur Ekker, present owner of Robbers Roost, showing them to Mrs. Parker Hamilton.

—PHOTO COURTESY OF PARKER HAMILTON, FLAGSTAFF, ARIZONA

turned to Montpelier, the newlyweds were long gone on a horseback honeymoon all over the West.

According to Matt's later stories, he and Tom would set up camp back in the woods, leave the girls there and go into town. After holding up the bank, they would return, move on and live the life of Riley for a few weeks. When funds ran low, they would strike again. Trying to rob the bank at Butte, Montana, they almost met their Waterloo, and one wonders what would have become of the two women in the lonely camp if the boys hadn't made it back for them.

Because this shook them up, they decided to go to North Poudre, Oregon, where Billy McCarty had moved from the La Sals, and go straight. They found a bad drought there and Billy's cattle ranch in difficulties. The bank was threatening to foreclose and, since the range was in such poor condition, Billy wasn't in a position to hang on much longer. He was ripe for a new line of business.

The boys showed him a lucrative new vocation: banditry. They held up a placer camp, making off with a bunch of gold nuggets. Much to Billy's dismay, he found he couldn't spend the money right away but had to hide it until the officials quit looking for certain identifiable nuggets. They hid the loot in a hole dug in the dirt floor of the chicken house.

A few months went by, and Billy's fifteen-year-old son, Fred, went to town for a few days, returning with new clothes and a wild tale of his spending spree in town. When questioned about what he had used for money, he said, "Oh, I had a few nuggets."

"Yes, and I know where you got them," Matt replied. "Mined them in your dad's chicken-coop." Fred admitted that he had, and they all laughed about it.

Matt tried to settle down in Oregon and be a rancher, particularly after his daughter, Mayda, was born. He had left too wide a swath and too plain a trail, though, and when the law closed in on him was forced to send Rose to her people who had moved to Salt Lake City.

It cost him all the money he had, several thousand dollars, for a lawyer, and even then he was forced to serve some time in the penitentiary. When he was released, he was more than ever determined to go straight, and remembered Diamond Mountain with homesick longing.

Meeting Rose in Rock Springs, Wyoming, they drove to Diamond, and Matt started ranching again. He spared no effort in developing his spread, even built a reservoir which is still in use today.

Rose was happy there, but bad luck struck them a blow again when she began to be troubled with pain and swelling in her knee. It was cancer. In a few months she had to have her leg amputated, and she died in Salt Lake City a year or two after their son Rex was born.

Just before Rex was born, Matt was involved in a serious shooting scrape. Butch had returned from the Wyoming Penitentiary and was organizing the Wild Bunch. He had always liked Matt, and from succeeding events, it is certain, felt a great loyalty to him.

Matt and Bill Wall (Silvertip) were in Vernal when a mining man, E. B. Coleman approached them. He said he had gone to Dry Fork to look for some copper showings,

and had been followed by three men from Vernal, Adon-
iram (Dick) Staunton, his brother Isaac (Ike) and Dave
Milton (Melton).

From here the stories got pretty well mixed up at the
trial, but that Coleman was not able to shake the three men
is certain. Some say he offered them $500.00 to leave him
alone, but Dave Milton said Coleman had defrauded his father and he was looking for revenge. It was also reported
that Coleman gave Matt Warner and Wall $500.00 (or
$100.00) to get rid of the three men. At any rate, Warner
and Wall rode back to the camp with Coleman.

They left town in the evening, planning, it was said, to
arrive at the camp at daybreak and take the three men by
surprise. Warner said that they lost their way in the dark
and camped, rising at daybreak and going to the camp,
with Coleman staying back out of range.

According to several accounts, Ike Staunton or one of his
associates fired first. Warner's horse was killed in the first
volley, putting Matt on the ground. As his horse was going
down, Matt grabbed his rifle and pistol and began firing.

Some accounts say all three were barricaded behind some
logs, ready for ambush. Others say that Ike Staunton
stepped out of the tent, heard horses approaching, began
firing when Matt appeared, killing his horse; that Matt
and Wall returned the fire, shooting into the tent and
seriously wounding Milton, who was still in bed; that Dick
Staunton stepped to the door of the tent to see what the
shooting was all about, was struck by a bullet and fell back
into the tent, badly wounded.

Ike Staunton and Matt each took protection behind a tree
and began firing at each other. Ike received a bullet in the
leg but, according to Matt's later stories, was not too greatly
incapacitated. Matt said that he was standing behind a
quaking aspen about eight inches through, so small that he
had to stand sidewise to have any protection. As long as he
stood there, Ike could not damage him, because the rifle
slugs would not go through the tree; the only way one would
was to have a hole through the bole and an expert marksman hit it dead center. However, Ike was a good shot, and
he had a repeating rifle. He fired one slug right on top of

another into the tree, driving a hole through. When Matt saw the bark begin to bulge on his side of the tree, he knew he would have to make different arrangements. That was Matt's story, told many years after.

At the time the fight was taking place, it is certain Ike would have scored a hit on Matt, but Wall fired at him, and the bullet cut the bridge of his nose and put him out of action.

Matt sent Silvertip back to Vernal for some kind of conveyance to carry the wounded men to town. He stayed and took care of them, and all three lived to get to town. Milton and Dick Staunton died in a couple of days, and although Ike lived, he was left a cripple.

These three men were well liked in Vernal. Generally the people in that area were incensed over this gunfight and its results. The papers were full of speculation and rumors. The law officers were faced with a real problem: The townspeople might release Warner and Wall and string them up, or the Wild Bunch might release them and spirit them out of the country. It seemed best to take them to Ogden, and that is what was done.

Butch and Lay camped at Uinta, in the mouth of Weber Canyon, and sent word to Matt they would liberate him. But he felt he had a good chance to get out of it and he decided to stand trial. Butch and Lay, it is said, robbed the Montpelier bank in Idaho on August 13, 1896, to get money to hire Douglas A. Preston, whom Butch believed in, to defend Matt. The reported retainer was $3,000.00. However, one of the Ogden papers reported an interview with Preston wherein he hotly denied this, stating that he had had his retainer ($1,000.00) long before the bank was robbed.

Discussion during the trial at Ogden seemed to point out that Coleman made a contract with Warner and Wall to kill the three interlopers and eliminate them. It was also pointed out that Ike Staunton began firing first.

Warner and Wall served time in the Utah State Penitentiary at Salt Lake City. Butch and Lay called on Rose and gave her money and helped her until she died.

Matt was whipped. He still had some old misdeeds hanging over him, and two small children to raise. When Frank Taylor of Salina offered to take the children, Matt reluctantly gave his consent. Rex was always delicate and died when he was eighteen, but Mayda grew up and married John Causer of Price, where she spent her life.

Matt got out of jail on January 21, 1900, when he was thirty-six years old. He was determined to go straight and he did. He lived for a time in Green River, Utah, and then moved to Price, where he was night marshal for several years before his death.

Matt knew all of the Wild Bunch, but with the exception of Tom McCarty, who had married his sister, he didn't ride with them much. In fact, from when he was sent to the Utah State Penitentiary in September of 1896 to his release in January, 1900, was the period the Wild Bunch did most of their daring holdups. He never participated in any holdup with Butch Cassidy after Butch's initiation, the Telluride Bank robbery, and was never with Elzy Lay. There is reason to believe from the stories told or printed about him that Matt was never actually at the Roost at all; he never definitely locates it.

However, it is said that after Butch and the Union Pacific officials failed to meet late in the spring of 1900, they hired Matt (gave him $175.00) to find Butch and tell him the deal was still on. He was trying to find his man, had traveled to Fort Bridger, when a telegram was handed him that the train had been robbed at Wagner, Montana, and although this was not on the Union Pacific, Butch was a participant, and it definitely put an end to their offer.

Maybe Matt didn't know exactly where the Roost was, but that was not the case with Joe Walker, next on our list. He spent a good deal of time there and was one of the Wild Bunch, riding on many of their raids. He spent his best years around the campfires and riding over the Roost Flats, finally coming to an outlaw's death on the Book Mountains above Green River when a posse followed him to Moonwater Spring and killed him—an event that definitely caused the boys to seek safer surroundings.

JOE WALKER

Joe Walker was about 35 or 40—old by the standards of most of the Wild Bunch, who were young and reckless—when he came into the country in the early '90s. He was small, but "all man," rather good looking and dark; a silent man as a rule, and one given to traveling alone most of the time. Like the rest of the stray cowboys hunting the shortest way into the eastern Utah area, he came down White Canyon and across the Colorado River at Dandy Crossing, hitting into the Henry Mountains first.

Dropping down onto the Burr Flats, he met his first rider, a boy herding the town milk cows. As was customary with small Mormon towns, Hanksville had its town herd grazing on the surrounding hills and watched over by one of the smaller boys. Jack Cottrell had the contract that summer, and his step-son, Bill Tomlinson, who was about 11 or 12, found the job of riding herd on the ornery old milk cows a dull, lonesome job. Any chance traveler who passed near enough, Bill stopped for a few words to kill the monotony of the day.

When he was hailed, Joe, having plenty of time, got off his horse to join Bill on the Brigham tea sand bump. He produced the "makin's" and they both rolled and lit a smoke. Bill was acting very grown up and "one of the fellows," so Joe played along.

Finding Joe a ready listener, Bill had a great deal to tell him: Who was going where and why. Oh, there was a lot about the town, too—who was expecting babies, what young people were going together, who was working for what outfit and how much he was getting.

The afternoon had waned by the time Bill had run down, and Joe, after helping him get his cow herd headed toward the home corrals, led his packhorse over under a cottonwood tree in Bull Valley and threw off camp. He needed to know about the country, and he decided he had found the right source.

It took Bill all summer to get Joe checked out, but by reading all the newspapers the boy brought and listening carefully, Walker knew enough about the people of Utah that he might have passed for an early settler. When he pulled out for Price in the first cool days of fall, the men he had come to see were not strangers to him.

Joe had come to Utah to claim his property, or so he said. If the story that comes from all the ranchers who knew him well be true, he had every reason to become an outlaw. He claimed that when his father had died in Texas, while Joe was just a baby, his mother had turned a considerable outfit over to her brother, Dr. Whitmore, to be cared for. During the late '60s or early '70s, he had moved the cattle to Arizona with his own, and settled at Pipe Springs on the "Arizona Strip" in the extreme northern part of the state.

There, he and his partner were killed by Indians, and his widow sold her rights to Pipe Springs to the Mormon Church, the water to be used for Tithing Herds.* She and

---

* In the early days of Utah, members of the Church of Jesus Christ of Latter Day Saints (LDS or Mormons) "tithed in kind" by paying into the church 10 percent of the increase of their herds. Thus, the Church soon found itself in the livestock business in a big way. These herds were handled as a company would have been managed, and some men worked most of their lives with the Tithing Herds, drawing wages for their labor.

her sons, George and Tobe, then moved to Salina, Utah, and finally into Carbon County, where they prospered and became one of the leading livestock and banking families of the state.

No accounting had ever been made to Joe's mother, and after her death Joe came to Utah to see what could be done. He followed the Whitmores into Carbon County to see what settlement he could make with them.

This was Joe's story—the Whitmores flatly denied either the relationship or the claim, and refused to have anything to do with Walker. He had no resources of either money or influence and, like most of his class at the time, knew little of and believed less in legal action. He was bitter, although people who knew him best liked him, and thought he was justified in his outlawry.

Joe spent several years around Price in various jobs while trying to get his cousins to divvy up. He worked for the Day brothers in Huntington, at a saw mill, but being a good rider and handy with a gun, he was soon among the cowpunchers again. He started to hound the Whitmores and made life so unbearable for them that it finally became necessary to hunt him down like a lobo wolf and exterminate him.

Ranchers who knew Joe might have been on his side, but that was not the case with the leading citizens of Price, who were friends and associates of the solidly entrenched, wealthy Whitmores. During the summer of 1895, the Price newspaper carried a writeup about Joe shooting up the town. This was not an uncommon occurrence, but Joe's escapade was given a great deal of publicity, and from that time on he was a marked man. He threw in his lot with the Robbers Roosters, although he was always more or less a loner, plying his horse-thieving and other depredations up and down the Owlhoot Trail traveled by the Wild Bunch.

One of the less publicized way stations on this trail was Florence Creek, a small stream flowing into the Green River from the east, above Green River, Utah. Jim McPherson, not knowing this, brought in a bunch of cows and set up an outfit there. He liked the stream, the good feed, and the encircling ledges and canyons. But he had hardly got his cabin built before he found he had lots of company. The Wild

Bunch had long used the pastures to rest their horses as they drove stolen stock from Wyoming to Texas and back again. Summertime was horse-stealing time, and this was a safe, out-of-the-way place to stay a few days and let their prizes fill up and rest.

McPherson figured if he protested he could be cleaned out overnight. He wanted no part of the Wild Bunch, and he saw that he could be caught pretty much in a squeeze. The time finally came when he had to do something about it. Shortly after he was married (he was on his way out to get married when he met the posse following Walker) he moved to the Heber area for several years. But when the outlaws had been cleaned out of the country, he returned to Florence Creek. There he raised his family, and finally sold the ranch to his son-in-law, Ray (Budge) Wilcox. It was bought in 1942 by the Government for inclusion in the Uintah Ute Reservation, when the boundaries were extended.

While he was running cattle in the Florence Creek area, McPherson did as most of the ranchers in the West did at that time—minded his business and accepted the casual traveler on his merits. Even though Joe Walker was tied in with the Wild Bunch and McPherson knew it, Joe stayed at the ranch often, and they became close friends.

On one trip out after supplies, the cattleman left Joe in charge of the ranch, making him promise faithfully to feed the stock and take care of things. During his stay in civilization, Jim heard about a saloon robbery at Thompson Springs that had all the earmarks of a Joe Walker job. But Jim knew where Joe was, and knew he was too far away to have done it.

McPherson returned to the ranch late at night, and Joe was all hospitality, jumping out of bed to light the lamp. The table was covered with candy, cigars, etc., from the saloon.

"Damn it, Joe," protested the stockman, "I told you if you were going to do things like that you couldn't stay here any more. It gives me a bad reputation."

"Jim, I don't know what you are talking about." Joe was aggrieved. "You made me promise to tend the stock, and I did. They've been fed and watered twice a day, even if it was early one evening and late the next morning—pretty damn early and late, in fact." Joe was being overly honest and shone with virtue. "But you didn't tell me what to do with my spare time."

One time Joe drove a bunch of horses to the pastures in Horseshoe Canyon at the Roost, worked the brands over, and left them there to heal. "Wet" horses were a constant risk while they were being traded off or sold, but when the brands had healed, it was generally safe enough to handle them. While he waited, he rode to Wyoming to look around and on the way back stopped at Florence Creek.

Jim was lonesome and glad to see him, and Joe, traveling light, was glad to turn his big black horse with the saddle bunch and rest a day or two, Jim, having "taken a likin'" to the horse, wanted to trade Joe out of him. There were two reasons why Joe didn't want to trade—the horse was too close to home to be safe for Jim, and there wasn't a horse on the ranch that Joe would have considered in a trade. He wished later, though, that he had left the horse.

A few days later he rode out onto the San Rafael Desert and bumped into a posse out looking around. It was quite a popular pastime with local farmers, deputy sheriffs and other small-time law officers to relieve the monotony of life with a camping trip to capture outlaws for the reward money. They always hoped to snag a lone bandit and almost scared each other to death with spooky precautions in regard to their dangerous prey. Though no one ever got an outlaw (Matt Warner tells how he sent a couple of these outlaw hunters back without their pants), this particular posse might have—with just a little more guts.

They recognized Joe and started a running gun battle, trying to shoot the horse. This they finally did, hitting it in the stifle and putting one hind leg almost out of use. The horse was ridden, however, by one of the finest horsemen around, and Joe managed to hold it up long enough to make the willows along the bank of the San Rafael. This was much better than the bald flats of the desert, and Joe settled in to wait. When he saw how badly the horse was wounded, his first act was to put a merciful bullet through the animal's brain.

The posse followed the blood trail to the edge of the willows, but were afraid to go any farther. True, not all of them would have come back, but five of them could have bagged one man, and the survivors would have had a nice reward to split. This wasn't good enough odds for the boys and they went home.

Joe watched them ride off, figuring they would return when it was dark, and spent the rest of the afternoon digging in behind the carcass of the black horse. Along about sundown he heard a horse coming down the trail snorting at the blood. Joe listened carefully, cocking his head first on one side then the other, and finally judged by the horse's wariness that it was loose. He spun out his rope and waited.

When the mustang came opposite Joe's fort, he raised up and instantly laid a loop around the throatlatch of the roan pony. Had the posse returned in the next hour, they would have had no trouble making a capture—Joe's attention was all taken up with his bronco-busting. Together the two of them plowed up the little clearing among the willows before the horse had been choked down, bridled, let up and broken to lead, sacked out and saddled. Usually this takes two or three days, but Joe was in a hurry.

When the moon rose that evening, it found a much subdued horse and a tired rider plodding across the sand dunes of San Rafael Desert toward the Roost.

Picking up his cached camp and rounding up his horses, Joe headed for Colorado. The little roan pony brought his $35 the same as the rest of the bunch when Joe hit the mines a few weeks later.

Joe, being alone so much, attracted another posse that summer. He was riding where the road follows along under a ledge just before reaching Granite when the posse, composed of Jack Cottrell, Rufe Stoddard, Oscar White, Oscar Beebe and Joe Bush, prowling the desert in their usual quest, came upon him. Joe waved them back but they were foolhardy and didn't go back, so he started shooting at them.

Perhaps the idea for western movies generated in some such brush with outlaws as this—where so many shots are fired but no one is hit. Don't make any mistake about the marksmanship of the Wild Bunch; they were not amateurs with a gun, but the best of them, the ones who lived long and were liked and respected, had no intention of shooting to kill.

There was a practical reason for this. They could rob trains, steal horses, hold up payrolls and create about enough opposition to make life interesting—but murder changed the whole picture. Tom McCarty found that out. After the bank holdup at Delta, Colorado, when the banker was killed, Tom never dared show up again and was a fugitive the rest of his life. Therefore, outlaws shot wild on purpose.

The posses didn't make a hit because they often got buck fever, and anyway most of them "couldn't hit a bull in the butt with a scoop shovel," as one fellow expressed it.

In the customary manner of the Wild Bunch, Joe didn't hit the bunched posse and they, although they followed him for about fifteen miles, didn't get close enough to get a decent shot. They just furnished entertainment for him as he went down Hell's Hole, across to the Dirty Devil River several miles above Beaver Box, across the river and out on the point north of Buck Canyon into the Roost.

During these years Joe managed to make "a whelty" around to Price now and then to keep the Whitmores apprised of his continuing and predatory interest in their affairs. They had splendid horses, although it wasn't that so much as it was the nuisance value of his depredations that was so satisfying to Joe and so unnerving to the Whitmores.

Tobe's wife had a particularly fine saddle horse, a little bay, that she valued highly. It and Tobe's top saddle horse were kept at a ranch south of Price, and somehow Joe found out about them.

One night he and Gunplay Maxwell stole these horses out of the stable and led them down the San Rafael River to Mexican Bend, below Swasey's Leap where the Robbers Roosters often camped. It was here a few years later that one of the changes of mounts was left for the Castle Gate holdup.

After sleeping for a while, the two started to get their

outfits ready to go on to the Roost, but some sort of argument developed and Gunplay got on his horse and pulled out. Joe decided to lay over one more night, not having any idea that Gunplay was headed for Price to tell the Whitmores where to find their horses.

Sheriff Allred of Carbon County picked up Sheriff Azariah Tuttle of Castle Dale (the horses were in Emery County) and rode for Mexican Bend. The two surprised Joe down on the river bank, where he'd gone for a bucket of water, and cut him off from the house and corrals.

Joe had dipped up his bucket of water and started back up the bank when he saw Sheriff Allred between him and the cabin, and outside the open door a horse with the reins trailing. He set the bucket down, retreated across the shallow stream quickly and quietly and climbed the south bank. He broke out of the fringe of willows and started up the canyon. If he could make the dim trail out of the ledged canyon, he might have a chance to get away.

Just as he entered the mouth of the canyon, he heard a shout from across the river, and in seconds both sheriffs had splashed across the stream on their horses in hot pursuit.

Joe ran up the canyon and made the trail, slugs bouncing off the rocks all around him. He was too busy to return the fire until he fell winded behind a rock about halfway up the talus slope. He drew down carefully and put a bullet through the leg of Sheriff Tuttle, who was in the lead. The lawman tumbled off his horse and rolled behind a rock big as a house. Allred rode behind the rock, taking the other horse with him.

"Now I'm in for it!" Joe muttered to himself. He looked up the trail; it was right in plain sight and he knew that he wouldn't have a chance.

"Joe, can you hear me?" One of the men shouted from behind the rock.

"Yeah, sure." Joe refused to add any further comment that might show worry about his situation.

"You better give up, Joe. We've come for you, and we don't aim to go back without you."

"I guess you'll have to come and get me, then." Joe was

eyeing the ledge. All the lawmen needed to do was split forces and while the wounded Tuttle kept him pinned to the trail, Allred could go back around the corner of the canyon, climb out afoot and move around on top until Joe was right under him, completely without cover. The rock he had fallen behind was good-sized, but not big enough to shelter him from above.

Just as he reached this conclusion, Allred broke from behind the rock, leading Tuttle's saddled horse and spurring fiercely while he leaned down against his horse's far side. Joe snapped a couple of shots, but missed the swiftly moving target.

He decided to make a run for it, but a couple of slugs ricocheting off the rock when he showed himself convinced him he'd better lay low a while anyway. Tuttle had missed him because he hadn't allowed for shooting uphill, but Joe knew the lawman would correct for that in the future.

A few minutes went by and Joe looked down the canyon to see Allred leaving with all the horses.

"Where the hell is Allred going?" he yelled to Tuttle.

"After help," came the answer. "I'm to keep you pinned right up there in the rimrock and, even with this slug in my leg, I can do that. Just don't try anything."

Joe settled back to marvel at the ways of lawmen. He had seven or eight hours at least, and with Tuttle crippled, he should be able to do something about his position in that length of time. The sun beat down on him and he flipped pebbles at a couple of little rock lizards that came out to look him over. One climbed up on the rock in front of him, did push-ups and looked ready to burst with curiosity. Joe grinned at his antics, and changed position.

A little stick, probably a limb off the cedar up on the hill above him, was gouging him in the back. He picked it up and started to throw it over the rock and down the hill. Suddenly he changed his mind and set to work, propping the stick against the rock while he searched his pockets for some string. Taking off his hat, he tied the buckskin string under the hat band. He knew well that such an old hand as Tuttle wouldn't be fooled by a hat thrust straight up on a stick.

He wanted to know just where Tuttle was behind the big rock. A small bush grew on the upper side of the rock, and the floods had built out a little sandbar below, which had grown up to grass and weeds. There were several shaly slabs on top of the main boulder, and probably Tuttle could find a shelf behind it to stand on and peer over the top.

Joe set the hat on the cedar limb, waggled the string experimentally and when he figured he had it about right, raised it slowly up above his shelter while he flattened himself and peered from a lower corner. As the hat cleared the rock, there was a flat *spang!* and a bullet caught the hat, jerked it off the stick and sailed it up the hill.

Joe had miscalculated. He had planned that if Tuttle shot the hat off he could hang onto the string, or that the hat would roll down and he could retrieve it. The hat stayed where it had fallen, ten feet above the rock.

Joe didn't even glance at it, the shot had come from the upper side of the rock where the bush grew. He threw four shots quickly into the bush.

"Good shootin', Joe, but I'm not there any more," Tuttle laughed.

"And it cost me a twelve-dollar hat to find that out," Joe admitted bitterly.

"You're going to miss that hat."

"Not too much, the more the sun gets over to the west, the more shade I'll have," Joe answered.

Suddenly he looked around the bottom of the rock again and surveyed the position of the law officer. "That's not the way it's going to be with you," he exulted. "You're about out of shade now, and this afternoon you're really going to get warmed up. The lower the sun gets, the better off I am, and the worse off you'll be."

Tuttle didn't answer, and Joe re-settled himself and took up lizard-watching again. An hour or so later, he took another careful look down the hill and found the little strip of shade had widened on his side of the big rock. Another hour dragged slowly by, and Joe, in spite of his discomfort without his hat in the blinding glare, had almost dozed when he heard:

"Joe, I guess you win. I can't take it any longer."

"What do you mean?" It didn't hurt to be certain.

"Well, I can't stand this sun any longer, and I'm about to choke to death. I'll let you go if you'll go get me some water. I couldn't make it back to the creek with this slug of yours in my leg."

Joe thought it over. It must be hotter than hell over on the other side of that rock, and on top of that, Tuttle must be pretty uncomfortable with the fever from his wound.

"All right, throw your guns out as far as you can, and I'll come down."

The spurts of dust kicked up by the guns flung from behind the rock had no more burst than Joe grabbed his hat and, slapping the dust out of it, put it back where it belonged. Sure felt good! Since there had been no activity from down the hill, Tuttle must be on the level.

While he ran lightly down the trail, Tuttle dragged himself around in the shade. As Joe went past, he stopped to look down at the wounded man.

"You are in bad shape, that's for sure," Joe remarked compassionately.

"You know it!" Tuttle agreed. "God, Joe, hurry that water up."

Joe gathered up the two guns just to be on the safe side, went on down the canyon to the stream, where he waded across and threw the guns back up on the farther bank. He picked up the bucket, emptied the warm water out of it, slopped back across the stream, dipping it full, and started back up the canyon. He picked up a rusty can on the way to use for a drinking cup and put it and the bucket down by the wounded officer.

"You've won again this time," Tuttle remarked after he had gulped down a couple of cans of water. "But don't brag, your time is coming."

"Probably," Joe agreed. "But it'll take better planning than you boys showed today to do the job."

"I know. I figured after Allred left that we should have just stayed right here and climbed above you and finished you off. But we were in a hurry, and didn't think of it then." He settled himself more comfortably and held up his hand. "Goodbye, Joe, take care of yourself."

"Sure will." Joe reached down and took the proffered hand. "Better luck next time. Don't try to follow me, I've got nothing to lose now."

Joe climbed out of the canyon onto the high ridge of the San Rafael Swell, and looked across the desert toward the Roost, settled his hat again on his sunburned forehead, and started the long hike.

Luck was with him. He had walked about two miles, when he dropped over into a swale and ran onto an old sorrel horse belonging to Buhr that he knew well. The horse was named Amos. He was stupid, gentle and old, and let Joe walk right up to him, a fact he tried to remember with kindness when Amos made rather poor time to the Roost. His old back was boney and rough, too, and all Joe had to guide him was the buckskin string he'd used on his hat behind the rock and his belt. This was not much of an outfit for a man who took as much pride in his trappings as did Joe Walker. But he managed to do better when he hit the Roost the next morning.

A few months later he helped with the Castle Gate holdup, cutting the telegraph wires and following the boys to Desert Lake, where he took the money over the mountain for them. This robbery aroused the countryside and made the lawmen determined to do something to quiet the far from flattering comments of the press all over the West. All the newspapers ran editorials about the shameful state of affairs. The Castle Gate holdup furnished the final goad and doomed Joe, who was already fair game for the Price officers.

He wasn't doing anything to ease the situation, either, coming and going as he pleased in spite of a price on his head. Finally he committed an assault on the Whitmores so daring that they were forced to act.

In the spring of 1898, after the Castle Gate holdup, he picked up a bunch of Whitmore cattle and started driving them down Price River, where it cuts Elliot Butte off the Book Cliffs. Billy McGuire, Whitmore's foreman, and Bud Whitmore, who was just a kid, followed him.

This bothered Joe. He hated Billy, anyway, so he waited in the willows after he had crossed the river, and as Billy's horse started struggling up the steep bank, jumped and caught it by the bridle. Holding the horse by the bridle with one hand, Joe reached over and before Billy knew what he was going to do, unbuckled the rider's cartridge belt, flipping the gun into the river and gave Billy a severe beating, still holding the horse. Taken unawares like he was, Billy made no showing at all.

When he had extracted a promise from Billy to go back and never follow a better man again, Joe turned to Bud and asked him if he cared for a helping of the same. Bud assured him that he didn't, and as Joe didn't recognize him as one of the hated Whitmores, he let the two go and went on about his business. He changed his mind about stealing the cattle; he turned them loose and went on toward Florence Creek alone.

The *Eastern Utah Advocate* of May 12, 1898, states that after the fracas, Joe took their outfits, but other accounts of the affair do not say so, and it seems reasonable to suppose he didn't, the pursuit was organized so quickly.

This exciting affair even crowded out the news of the Spanish American War for a few issues. The *Advocate* states further:

> It (the posse) is composed of J. Wesly Warf, than whom there are none braver; Jim Inglefield, whose war record is away up and whose carrying capacity has never been determined; Sheriff Tuttle of Emery County who knows how it feels at the front when Walker is on the "Roost"; Sheriff Allred, who will scrap if given a chance; Tobe Whitmore and Jack Gentry, both good men, and stayers and Jack Watson who is reputed to be a first class man in such emergencies. The above celebrities make up the distinguished party which will seek to bring Joe Walker in. Should they succeed the country will be glad, but should Walker spring up in some unnoticed place and get the drop on the gang, he could open up a hardware store with the stock of guns he would take as a "prize."

When the posse reached Woodside on the Price River, Sheriff Allred sent Inglefield and McGuire into Woodside with dispatches. Joe Bush and a rancher named Coleman came back with them, and the group then proceeded down Price River to its confluence with the Green River, then up the Green. They camped that night on the Price River somewhere near its mouth.

About the middle of the next forenoon they were wending their spooky way up the banks of the Green River when they rounded Red Point and rode right into a horseman. After several shots at him, the posse recognized Jim Mc-Pherson, riding a raw bronc that had stampeded up the sidehill.

Jim wanted no part of a posse following Joe Walker. He tried to make this clear to them, even telling them where he was headed—out to Scipio to get married. Besides, he couldn't afford to take sides against the Wild Bunch; but the posse pointed out he couldn't afford to take sides with the outlaws, either.

The argument got a little heated, and Jim finally decided he would save time by going back with them, at least to the crossing of the Green. The river was booming full, and Jim kept a boat at the crossing. It was his custom to row the boat across the river, leading a horse behind it. This, to the horse, was a tremendous improvement over swimming loose, as it kept his head out of the water and actually towed him behind the boat.

Jim had left a young fellow, who had just wandered in, to do the chores. The boy wasn't any brighter than needs be, and Jim didn't think it was a good idea to let him drown himself, so had given him strict orders that under no conditions was he to take the boat on the river. The last thing he had said, as he stood with his reins in his hand and his horse dripping and spooky at his side, was that the boy wasn't even to show up if he heard a hail. Let anyone who came up, either go back or cross at his own risk. The boy had looked stupidly up from the boat, oars poised, and agreed to do just that.

It was late in the afternoon when the group approached the crossing. Some of the men looked at the river and, knowing its unpredictable currents and silt-laden power, voted to return. Sheriff Allred agreed with them, but gave a halloo just for good measure. McPherson, standing back, was taking no part.

The boy came running down the bank, jumped into the boat and shoved off, too enthralled with the prospect of someone to talk to to remember Jim's warnings. He was considerably cowed when he got to the shore, ran the boat in and looked up into Jim's blazing eyes.

Jim fixed supper for the bunch and, as they were eating, heard them start all over again on where Joe was likely to be, and maybe they just better go back. Tobe insisted on going on, at least to the Wyoming state line, and they discussed how far it was. The chore boy carried in wood and water, and started to say something, glancing fearfully at Jim. McPherson's threatening look shut off his information, and he went back out to the saddle shed and stretched out on his bed.

The sheriff wandered past a while later, on his way to the corral to check on the horses. He stopped to talk to the boy, and hit pay dirt with almost the first try.

"Oh, Jim knows where Joe is, all right," the boy stated. "He knows they usually camp at Moonwater Spring. And I know it, too. I can do even better than that."

"That so? Here, have a smoke."

"Sure, I went up there this afternoon, but don't tell Jim, he'd skin me alive. I know just where they are, all four of them, and I can show you if you won't tell Jim."

"We won't tell Jim, and we might be able to make up a little reward for you. How would that be?"

"That will be all right. I'll go show you. I'll ride my own horse, and you give me the money, and I'll just go on straight out of the country. Sure you won't tell anybody where you got your help? Not Jim, or any of them outlaws?"

The sheriff promised solemnly and went back to the house to tell the posse to saddle up, they were riding farther that night. Although some of them grumbled, they got ready and rode away.

It was too late for Jim to go anywhere so he chored around the ranch until dark, and shortly after that he and the boy turned in, Jim in the house and the boy in the saddle shed. Jim didn't sleep well, but even at that he didn't

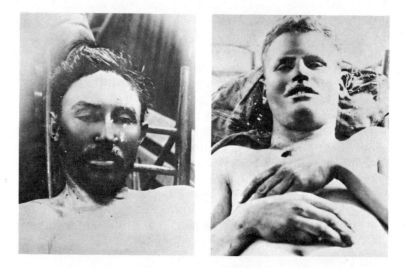

LEFT: Joe Walker, after he was killed. Note someone's arm supporting his head for the photograph.

—PHOTO COURTESY OF MRS. JUNE MARSING, BERYL, UTAH

RIGHT: Johnny Herring, who was killed with Joe Walker, photographed before burial. Note the bullet hole at the base of his neck.

—PHOTO COURTESY OF MRS. JUNE MARSING, BERYL, UTAH

hear the horse leave in the middle of the night.

About an hour before daylight the posse, after having slept as they could in the crisp May night, mounted stiffly and followed the guide to about 600 yards from where Joe was camped. Leaving their horses there the men approached very quietly and surrounded the camp. The bed in which Walker and a young fellow by the name of Herring were sleeping was pointed out to the sheriff by the boy, who then withdrew, having received all the money the posse had on them as a reward.

Just before daylight all men who live in the open awaken. There is a rustle of Mother Earth, a breath of awareness, a dawn breeze, all so subtle that only those attuned can catch it. Joe stirred, and the posse poured a hail of lead into the bed before he knew what had hit him. His gun was under the pillow, but he never even reached for it. He was killed instantly by a shot in the head, but received several other bullets, some of them carrying cloth from the quilts into the wounds, as later examination showed. Naturally, he would be shot up considerably with nine men pouring lead into one small bed roll. Eight men, rather—the newspapers of the time seemed to think editorially that Joe Bush, in spite of his tough reputation, took very little part in the actual shooting.

Great was the jubilation when the posse reached Thompson, Utah, with the two bodies, for everyone believed they had killed Walker and Butch. The posse had come out by Thompson to avoid crossing Green River again. Walker had been alone when he had been driving the Whitmore cattle, but it was believed that he had rendezvoused with Butch at Moonwater Spring, where the posse made the kill.

Some of the men were in favor of cutting off the heads of the outlaws to serve as a warning to the rest of the Wild Bunch, but were overruled by more responsible men among the group.

The newspaper at Vernal doubted that the second man was Butch, and stated that if one of the captured outlaws was Leigh (Lay), he was well known in Vernal, and had a wife living near there.

The posse and bodies returned by railroad from Thompson to Price, where a hearing was held for Mizzoo Shultz and Sang Thompson, the other two men that the boy had told the posse were also camped at Moonwater Spring. So exact had been his information that their bed had received no attention from the posse, and neither man was even scratched. They proved they were just wandering cowboys and had camped with the outlaw the night before, as had the boy who was killed with Joe, Johnny Herring.

Mizzoo Shultz and Sang Thompson were released, but all the horses the boys had in their possession were brought into Price, and just sifted around to different ranchers. Jim Liddell, a local stockman, told me many years later that he had ridden one of them all winter while working for Fausetts—a big, dark bay horse, weighing about a thousand pounds and a good son-of-a-gun.

The two bodies were buried on Sunday, outside the grave-yard at Price. The graves are now included in the enlarged cemetery but are still almost unmarked. The body of Herring was dug up on Monday, so that Sheriff Ward of Evanston, Wyoming, could state whether or not it was Butch, having known Parker well when he was in the penitentiary in Wyoming. Sheriff Ward stated positively that the body was not Butch Cassidy.

Mizzoo Shultz just seems to have disappeared, but Sang Thompson returned to Thompson and wrote to Lew Webb of Buffalo, Wyoming, asking him to forward some money to him. His business in the country was to look around for cattle to buy, and he and Tom Dilly planned to make a deal with Jim McPherson.

He received the money, saddled up one morning and started up Thompson Canyon, but was never heard from again. There is a story whispered that Tom lay out in the rocks and killed him, burying the body in a box, where it was later discovered wearing the same California wool pants and shirt that Ballard at the store in Thompson had sold Sang. The head was gone, so there could be no positive iden-tification.

Court records of the time bear no mention of a coroner's hearing, nor any other reference to the finding of a body, and nothing was ever published in the newspapers about it, so one wonders. There is no doubt, however, that when Tom Dilly bought Jim McPherson's cattle, he must have ob-tained the money somewhere besides earning it, and Sang Thompson never appeared again.

Tom moved the cattle across the Green River and threw in with Dowd and Forrester, two financiers who thought they were going to get rich, because Tom was going to "steal them rich." That's what he told them, but there was a slip-up.

TOM DILLY

Tom Dilly had made himself almost as unpopular with the Webster City Cattle outfit on Hill Creek, as Joe Walker had made himself in Price, and for the same reason. Not that Tom had a grudge, or that he preyed on Webster City any more than he did anyone else—they just had more to lose. He just couldn't keep his hands off other people's property.

Horace Allred, an old cattleman, remembers that one time when he was a kid he and Tom were riding along in the fall during a cold rain. Horace was particularly uncomfortable without chaps.

"Where's your chaps, Mormon?" Tom asked him.

"I haven't got any," Horace replied.

"In about two miles you will have," Tom prophesied.

When they reached the place, Tom gave his bridle reins to "Mormon" to hold while he scrambled up the hillside, returning presently with a new pair of chaps previously stolen from someone and cached in the rocks. It was said he would cheerfully give you the shirt off his back, and steal your watch while you donned it.

Tom Dilly was a tall, exceedingly thin man with curly black hair and snapping black eyes. He played a mouth harp (harmonica) all the time, joked and laughed a great deal, and was always popular around the cow camps. He used to visit the lonely ranches—the ones 'way out back of nowhere—and all the people enjoyed having him drop in. Many a discouraged heart took new hope after a visit from Tom.

During his time, Woodside, Utah, was the headquarters for the cattle country east of Price and was an important shipping point. A family named Warner lived on a ranch on Price River above Woodside, and Tom spent a lot of time there, because they had a parlor organ and Mrs. Warner played well. Tom always called her his second mother. One of the little girls, Martha, remembers him. She grew up to marry Bill Tomlinson, who spent his childhood at the Roost when his stepfather, Jack Cottrell, was foreman for J. B. Buhr. She liked Tom, and enjoyed his presents of candy and toys, even if he did tease her unmercifully.

Tom would go out of his way any day to "put up a job" on someone. Sometimes the hoax was rather elaborate, but sometimes it just fell in right for him to slicker someone.

One time he decided to take some chickens to his ranch on Range Creek above Woodside. He often stayed at a place in Woodside that kept guests, and it is likely that he got the idea for the practical joke from the nice flock of chickens this woman kept. He bought some scrawny old hens somewhere and brought them down and asked her if she would keep them for him until he could get around to take them out on the range. She agreed to do it, and Tom went back to camp.

On his next trip to Woodside he brought a coop tied on the top of a pack, and stayed all night at this place with the idea of taking his chickens back early the next morning. The woman's husband offered to get up and help him catch his before the hens came off the roost, which gave Tom a little start. Then he recalled that the husband wasn't overly ambitious and was relieved when the man relaxed as Tom assured him he could manage.

When he went out in the cool dawn to collect his fowl, he

got the correct number, all right, but they were fine Rhode Island Red hens. He took off for the hills, chuckling as he thought of the reaction of the woman when she went out and found his dung-hill chickens instead of her nice hens. He knew she would blow sky-high, and he thought it was funnier than hell.

When he returned a couple of weeks later, he thoroughly enjoyed the tongue lashing he got, then said, "But Ma, you want me to have real good chickens up at the cow camp, don't you?" Then paid her twice what her hens were worth.

Tom stayed with Jim McPherson on Florence Creek several winters. One spring, as he got ready to ride away for the summer, he said, "Jim, I've stayed here with you from time to time and never paid a cent. So this winter I've fixed it right with you. I've been branding Webster City Cattle Company calves for you all winter." And he laughed heartily.

Jim agreed it was all right, not to think a thing about it. He laughed, too. But later it dawned on Jim that maybe he'd better look the range over before the Webster City cowboys got out on the spring roundup. One day he made a *pasear* down over their range. Sure enough, Tom had been plenty busy; there were lots of big calves wearing Jim's brand—following Webster City cows. Jim rode on down to headquarters and got it straightened out before he was hanged as a cow thief, knowing well that Tom wasn't losing any sleep over it.

Tom had come into the Roost area on horseback from Texas after killing a fellow at a dance. They had both admired the same girl, but neither had actually been the winner; the other fellow got killed and Tom had to leave the country.

He ambled north, working a few days here and there, but mostly just riding chuckline until he hit the plateau country above Grand Junction, Colorado. When he asked Bill Kinney, one of the ranchers, for a job, Bill told him he was full handed, but gave him a letter to his brother Dan, foreman for the Webster City Cattle Company, north and west of there.

Tom rode on over. Dan didn't need a man, either, but

could use a chore boy. When clean-shaven, Tom looked like a big stripling of a boy. It wasn't long until they found this smooth-faced lad was a long way from being a mere boy, and Tom was promoted to cowboy.

About that time, a fellow by the name of Fullerton took over the management of Webster City Cattle Company, which was owned by rich Easterners. On the day he got to the ranch, Tom was shoeing a horse, and Fullerton ventured to give the youngster some advice. Dilly was having a little trouble, all right, but he resented the advice and when Fullerton, who didn't know him, persisted, Dilly worked him over with his sixshooter. One of the cowboys, Sam Jenkins, came up to interfere, and Dilly took him on, also, leaving them both somewhat contused and a whole lot wiser. From that time on he hated Jenkins, and when Jenkins was murdered Tom was immediately suspected.

Flat Nose George Curry came into the country that winter, too, although not for the first time, and threw in with Tom at the Webster City bunkhouse. They worked that whole winter shoving cattle across Green River onto the Range Valley side where they skinned out the V of the Flying V brand ⌄ , pulled the sides together and sewed up the hide with whang-leather string. When the brand had healed in a couple of months, the string was removed, the scar used for the bottom part of a T, with the "wings" on the Flying V making the cross bar on top. Tom used this ⊤ for his brand. In the spring, they had quite a sizable bunch of cattle left over after selling beef all winter to the Wasatch Stores at Sunnyside.

Flat Nose wasn't interested in setting up a ranch, but Dilly was, and in the spring bought out Jim McPherson's cattle. With the help of Flat Nose, he moved them across the river. While they were gathering the cattle west of the Hill Creek area, Sheriff Tyler and Sam Jenkins were killed in the Book Cliffs to the south of them. Although the newspapers of the time did not come right out and say so, it was commonly supposed that Tom was the killer, and the posse followed the two men to the Green River, where Flat Nose was mistakenly killed for Dilly.

The Moab *Times-Independent* (at that time the *Grand Valley Times*) gives the story in its issue of June 1, 1900 as follows:

KILLED BY OUTLAWS
Sheriff Jesse Tyler and S. F. Jenkins Murdered on the Book Cliffs

The residents of Moab were inexpressibly shocked and startled last Sunday about noon when word was received here from Thompson that Sheriff Jesse Tyler of Grand County, and a member of the posse, Sam Jenkins, were killed by outlaws. The killing took place about 42 miles above Thompson in the Book Mountains.

The posse had been out in that country for the past three weeks looking for some cattle rustlers that are badly wanted.

The story of the killing as told by Deputy Sheriff Day who was only about fifty yards away when the shooting occurred is as follows:

The posse had divided, one under Sheriff Preece of Vernal leaving the Grand County group. The Tyler posse had ridden about half an hour when they discovered a camp they believed was Indians. Tyler and Jenkins turned west toward it to investigate. They dismounted and approached the camp, which was among some willows, leaving their rifles on their saddles. When within a few yards of the outlaws, Sheriff Tyler spoke to them, saying, "Hello, Boys."

The reply made could not be heard by Deputy Sheriff Day, but immediately after it was made, Sheriff Tyler and Jenkins turned toward their horses, evidently having discovered their mistake. As soon as their backs were turned, the outlaws shot them through the back, the bullets coming out of their breasts, killing them instantly.

Mr. Day was a witness to the killing, but was in such a position that he could offer no assistance. As soon as they were killed, he started for assistance when the outlaws turned their guns on him, shooting twice but missing him.

Mr. Day then started in search of Sheriff Preece and posse of four men who were three miles away. As soon as he found them, they decided to come for assistance as there was supposed to be quite a number of outlaws in the party, they having about twenty horses with them.

They left the bodies of Sheriff Tyler and Jenkins where they fell and came to Thompson, arriving at 11 o'clock Sunday morning.

Upon the arrival of Deputy Day at Thompson word was wired to Governor Wells who sent a posse from Salt Lake to assist posses from Moab and Price in the search for the outlaws. Sunday morning it was learned that the outlaws had passed the Turner ranch, about 20 miles farther north, where they had taken fresh horses. Sunday night Messrs. Fullerton and King brought the bodies of the dead men to Thompson. A posse of 11 left Thompson Monday morning with Day and Westwood and in the afternoon a posse of 15 left with Sheriff Preece to follow up the trail. Sheriff Howell and posse of Salt Lake and Allred of Carbon are with the latter.

The lawmen were on the prowl for one reason only—to get Tom Dilly and Flat Nose, with some stolen cattle if possible. This killing made the excuse for following these two boys much stronger, in fact almost strong enough to cover the killing of Flat Nose by Doc King, Webster City Cattle Company's foreman. The name of Tom Dilly was whispered abroad in the land—but the migrant outlaws were never followed a mile. However, it was well known they had gone on through the country, and Tom Dilly's extermination had to be postponed. Besides, he was out of Webster City territory.

After turning his cattle loose at Range Creek, Tom rode down into Sunnyside, where he heard for the first time about Tyler and Jenkins. An old Irish coal miner asked him if he was Tom Dilly, and when Tom admitted that he was, the miner warned him to leave. A posse was forming to hang him for the killing of the Grand County sheriff.

Tom could see some fellows mounting up in the unmistakable form of a mob down the street, and ran to the Tid-

well Butcher Shop, where he borrowed a rifle. His horse
was tired, so he quickly threw his saddle on a big brown
horse belonging to Uncle Lou Benton, and made a run for it
up Sunnyside Canyon.

The mob was so close by this time that they cut him off
the trail, and forced him up the side of the wash that
pinched off into a ledge. He jumped his horse eighteen
feet (men measured it later) across the wash, and got away.
However, in the jolt, when the brown horse landed after the
jump, he dropped his rifle, and there certainly wasn't time to
stop and get it.

The trail up Sunnyside Canyon is almost straight up the
mountain side for about four or five miles, and Tom crowded
the old horse unmercifully. Topping out, he came into Jack
Chew's cow camp and asked to borrow a rifle. Jack wanted
to know what for, seeing the condition of the horse, and
Tom said he had seen a deer. He took the rifle back to the
top of the trail, but the lynch mob had given up.

Tom hid out in the hills for a few days, then sent Murray
Kessler, one of the Chew's cowboys, into town to see how
things looked. Murray learned that people had decided Tom
wasn't their man, so he and Murray and couple of other
boys of their stamp made a trip into Salt Lake City for a
week or two of "sporting around with the girls."

There was a place for a man as tough as Tom Dilly working for Dowd and Forrester on the Big Springs Ranch. The
ranch was just below Sunnyside, at the foot of the mountain,
and in Range Valley. For one thing, Tom was already in
the country, and they knew his reputation. It was going to
be a lot easier to keep an eye on him if he was on their
side. They had been having trouble with sheep, too, and
Tom might be just the man to handle that situation. Knowing that if he was running a brand in the country, he
would get more of their calves than they did, they offered
him a partnership in their Patmos Head Land and Cattle
Company, which Tom bought, after selling his cattle. Too,
he offered to "steal them rich."

Tom's efforts to handle the sheep situation turned out to
be pretty expensive. He ran unto a herd just north of Willow
Springs and learned that the herder wanted to go to town

for the 4th of July, but the boss hadn't sent out a replacement. Tom offered to look after the sheep while the fellow went in to celebrate.

A man named Chipman had a herd in that locality, and Tom offered to sell him a hundred head of this other fellow's sheep for a dollar a head, thinking that it would at least start a range war, if not bring on legal action. But Chipman was wily, and asked that the sheep be put into a corral with his earmark already on them. He had no money with him, but promised to pay Tom later.

The legal action never did develop, and Chipman refused to pay Tom the $100. The money wasn't so important, but it irked Tom to be bested by a sheepherder. Chipman got cocky, and moved his herd in on Tom's horse pasture around his camp, which was really asking for trouble.

There was so much legal action over what transpired, and so many stories told, that it is almost impossible at this late date to discover exactly what did occur. However, the story most told, and the most logical sounding one is this:

Tom was watering his horse at a spring when he saw Chipman and a Mexican herder, coming in with their packstring, Chipman leading a pack mule with his water kegs to take water for the camp. Tom remembered with bitterness that the camp was out about a mile on the bench, right where he had been in the habit of turning out his saddle horses to graze.

When Chipman got to the waterhole, Tom was spoiling for trouble and jumped him about the $100, also mentioning the horse pasture. Chipman said he wasn't going to pay the money and he didn't give a damn about the horse feed. Furthermore, he could shoot as fast as the notorious Tom Dilly, and he reached for his handkerchief in his back pocket. He wasn't armed.

The Mexican left at once, not even waiting to see where Dilly's one shot landed, reporting as he fled through Sunnyside that there had been a shooting at the spring.

Chipman fell from his horse, and Tom didn't have to dismount to see he was at last "a good sheepherder—a dead one." Turning his horse, he rode down the canyon, playing his harmonica. He met some fellows, including a doctor, in

a buckboard rocking along over the rough trail, and assured
them they were bringing the proper conveyance, although
they wouldn't need the sawbones.

He resumed his journey down the canyon, taking up the
tune on the mouth harp where it had been interrupted. He
swung off his horse at the store in Sunnyside and went in.
Buying a box of strawberries, he swung up to a seat on the
counter, dangling his legs, and ate the berries off the point
of his knife blade. He closed his knife, paid for the berries
and strolled outside. There wasn't anybody on the street,
he noted idly, as he stepped off the porch, and mounted his
horse to ride on down to his headquarters at Big Spring
Ranch.

This was one of the oldest and best ranches in the country, built around a big spring of amber colored water that
gushed from the bottom of a shallow wash. This water had
been used to irrigate fields and furnish water for cattle
belonging to Scott Elliot, who had settled on it first. He was
an Englishman, who came to America to make his fortune,
but the accounts of him are so varied and contradictory that
it is impossible to find out who or what he and his wife
were, or what became of them. Some say that she died at
the Big Spring Ranch. In any case, he had leased the ranch
to Dowd and Forrester about a year before Dilly came
along.

Dilly was eating dinner when Mr. Rasmussen, constable
at Sunnyside, came down to make an arrest. Tom walked
out into the yard when he rode up and asked if he had a
posse.

"No," said Rasmussen, "I haven't even got a gun."

"Come on in then," Tom answered, impressed with the
lawman's courage, "and as soon as I change clothes, I'll go
back with you."

They went on up past Sunnyside, and he didn't give up
his gun until they got to Price. He was sent to Provo for
safekeeping, and was cleared (as he fully expected to be)
at the preliminary hearing.

The Chipmans were a prominent Utah family, and although they took their sheep out of the Sunnyside area,
they demanded more action. Public opinion backed them,

and a grand jury was impaneled shortly to try to find another indictment against Dilly; the second verdict declared, also, there was no cause for action. The Mexican one Arthur McClure had drifted on down to Green River, where he was carrying mail from Green River to Hanksville. He was never called as a witness, but it is doubtful he could have added much to the testimony. Tom stuck with the story that he thought Chipman was going for his gun, and shot in self-defense. But the Chipmans demanded more than that, and it cost the Patmos Head Land and Cattle Company $40,000 to get an acquittal.

That fall the 〒C (PHC for Patmos Head Land and Cattle Company) shipped a trainload of cattle to Kansas City under Tom's care. This was a good portion of their holdings, but they had some debts to clear, and it took money to run an outfit of that size.

In the roundup, Tom just gathered all the cattle he ran across, and the local stockmen set up a howl about the number of their animals he had in the pens ready to go. Particularly insistent were the Tidwells, Frank and Keem, who had about sixty head of big steers they were planning to ship that fall. They openly declared they were going down to the shipping pens and cut out their steers.

Tom went to call on them, taking Keem a new Stetson hat as a gift. "I need them steers of yours to make up a trainload," Tom told them. "Why don't you let them go, they're gathered now, and you won't have to ride for them? And you'll get just as much out of them as the rest do out of theirs."

This made sense. The Tidwells had other irons in the fire, so they went along with him—and Tom made his word good to them.

Forrester and Dowd were no fools. They knew Tom was tough and crooked, and therefore they protected their interests by fixing the contract so that the check could not be cashed unless there were two of the partners' signatures on it. Tom ribbed them about it, but they went ahead and carried the deal through that way, and Tom left with the cattle. When he got to Kansas City, he called them, saying, "What do you think of bringing back some registered Hereford bulls?"

Cattlemen were just beginning to ship in pure-bred bulls to improve the quality of their herds, and Forrester wanted to be progressive. He released the check, and he and Dowd sat back and waited for the bulls to arrive—and waited and waited and waited. They finally started to investigate, and couldn't find either their money or Dilly and they never did. They got out of their cattle exactly the same amount as did the Tidwells.

During World War I, Lee Bryner from Price, while stationed in England, contracted pneumonia. He got steadily worse, and was finally moved to the death ward. One of the nurses there recognized the name, and with her interest and special care he finally pulled through. She was a Miss Winters from Mount Pleasant, Utah, and felt obligated to give a fellow Utahan extra care. When Lee got well, they went out a few times, and one evening at a dance at the Selfridge Amusement Hall, he met an English friend of hers, a Miss Dilly. After they got better acquainted, she told him her father had lived in Utah and invited Lee out to dinner.

He met her father, a tall rawboned elderly man who was eager to know something about Jack Moran, Tobe Whitmore, Billy Maguire and other oldtimers, some of whom had died in the intervening years. Although he never did come right out and admit his connection with the country, Lee could remember enough of the old stories to be able to place a man still named Tom Dilly.

Dilly was well-to-do, living in comfort on the money he had made in South America, run up from the stake he had taken out of the PHC. He had proved his old prophecy—he had been smart enough and tough enough to steal at least one member of the company rich. And his memories of the days when he and Flat Nose stole cattle from the Webster City Cattle Company, before Flat Nose was shot in his stead, must have made his old age nearly as spicy as his youth had been.

Thompson Springs, as it looked when the Wild Bunch used to outfit there before going into the Book Cliff area and Florence Creek.

—PHOTO BY MC CORMICK, PROBABLY IN 1901;
COURTESY OF MAJOR A. P. BALLARD, THE KNOLLS, ENGLAND

FLAT NOSE GEORGE
AND
THE CURRY BOYS

Flat Nose George was born George Sutherland Curry in
Prince Edward Island, Canada. The family migrated to
Nebraska, settling at Shadron, where Flat Nose spent his
childhood. In his late thirties he drifted west and threw
in with his nephews, John, Lonny and Orion (Kid) Curry,
who used the name Harvey Logan, also.*

Flat Nose George was a big man, weighing close to 190
pounds. He was light complexioned and he had a peculiar
nose, flat-bridged, yet with a point—not a knob—on the
end of it. He always said he had been kicked in the face by
a horse, but no one ever knew if it was one of his jokes or
the truth. It was plain that there had been some alteration,
probably violent, to his manly beauty.

---

* Author's note: It was long my belief that the Currys were John,
Lonny and Orion, and that Harvey Logan was a cousin, although
they used the name Logan sometimes and he occasionally used their
name. In some of my old notes, both Kid Curry and Harvey Logan
are listed on different exploits; however, I find that I'm the only one
with this idea, and I could be mistaken. I'm not trying to "make"
history, only to record it.

He spent several years in the Utah area, off and on. One fellow recalls, the first time he ever saw Flat Nose, he was laid out dead drunk under a cottonwood tree in Hanksville, with his sixshooter on the ground by his side. The natives were standing around talking about him, and wishing they had the nerve to take him in and collect the $1,000 reward posted for his capture.

While he was extremely active in Montana and Wyoming, he had a pretty good reputation in Utah—aside from the company he kept. About the only run-in he ever had with the Utah law was when he and Charley Lee from Torry drove a cow of Blackburn's to San Rafael and sold it. Blackburn had them both arrested and put under bond, with Preston Nutter going Flat Nose's bond. They were to appear for the same term of court for trial, and Flat Nose (Pete Logan at that time) did not appear. Nutter did. The court demanded that Nutter produce his man, or forfeit bail, and gave him a limited time to do it. Lee was convicted of stealing the cow, and served time.

After Lee was sentenced, Logan came in and gave himself up. When the trial opened, and the judge learned that Lee was already serving time for the theft of one single cow, he threw the case out of court.

Flat Nose then drifted north, where the Curry boys had established themselves in Wyoming. John, the eldest of the boys, had taken up a ranch near Hole-in-the-Wall among the foothills of the Big Horn Mountains. This ranch served as a cover for the cattle-rustling operations of Flat Nose and Butch Cassidy after they teamed up.

The Currys moved north into Montana and settled in the Little Rockies, with Landusky as their outfitting point. Here, under the name of Logan, they set up their usual operations, occasioning some protest from the contributing ranchers. W. H. Winters was one of these, and he swore out a warrant for John Logan for cattle stealing. The Logans sent word they would eliminate him at the first meeting, so Winters "heeled himself" and, when he met the brothers, shot John.

After the trial of Winters, wherein Pike Landusky gave evidence that freed him, Harvey Logan swore vengeance on Landusky.

While he was known at the Roost as Orion or Kid Curry, Harvey Logan mostly carried the name Harvey Logan in the north, although the name Kid Curry crops up there, too. When he went to South America, it was under the name Kid Curry, rather than Harvey Logan. This dual identity seems to reach deeper than geographical location—Kid Curry was always well liked, but the name Harvey Logan evokes a chill even today.

Harvey Logan was always a killer and would wait for years to even the score with someone. With the exception of the banker at Delta shot by Billy McCarty, practically every killing laid at the door of the Wild Bunch was committed by Harvey Logan. It took several years for him to get around to Winters, but he waited only a few months to get Landusky.

Landusky was host to the surrounding ranchers at a party and dance at his ranch. Festivities were in full swing when the Logans (including Flat Nose George and perhaps one or two more of the Wild Bunch) rode up to the ranch house and entered in a group. The guests stepped back at the entrance of these grim, armed men, and Landusky started down the center of the room to see what they wanted.

Harvey shot him in cold blood, the group whirled, ran for their horses and, mounting up in seconds, got away. This made them outlaws, and they hunted up Butch Cassidy, Elzy Lay, Harry Longabaugh (the Sundance Kid) and others, openly moving into the bank-robbing and train-holdup class.

They had known Butch in Wyoming, and even before he joined them at John Curry's ranch near Hole-in-the-Wall, Flat Nose and Butch had worked as cowboys, Butch for the Pitchfork ⤙ and Flat Nose for the Bar FS FS . Also working on the Bar FS at that time was Harry Longabaugh, who had been named the Sundance Kid after he shot up the town and landed in the local clink for a stretch.

In 1897, Harvey Logan, Walt Putney, Tom "Peep" O'Day and Willie Roberts (called Indian Billy, although he was a Mexican from New Mexico) laid plans to rob the bank at Dickerson, North Dakota. They didn't like the set-up when they gathered to do the job, and when Roberts told them about the Belle Fourche, South Dakota, bank, 300 miles

south of there, they thought it would be an easier job. They
moved on down there, Curry (Logan) went in and looked
the job over and decided it was a cinch.

They camped out about twenty miles from town, and on
a day late in June, 1897, rode into Belle Fourche, tieing
their extra horses in a grove of timber just outside town.
Dismounting in front of the bank, they handed their bridle
reins over to Peep O'Day to hold, and entered the bank.

The robbery went off strictly according to schedule, and
the men broke from the bank, everybody grabbing his horse
and mounting up. O'Day just stood by, shaking. Putney
told him to get on his horse and come on; Peep lost his
nerve and ran back of a saloon while the gang raced out of
town. Had Logan noticed him, he undoubtedly would have
promptly eliminated the hazard of Peep O'Day, but he was
out in the lead and didn't miss the defector. O'Day cowered
in the alley until the sheriff came along and put him in jail,
where he hastened to tell everything, naming names and
divulging future plans. He was later moved to the jail at
Deadwood, South Dakota.

The rest of the outfit headed for Hole-in-the-Wall, but
the law was pretty much alerted, and the fellows turned
south to Powder Springs and southern Wyoming, where
they split up. Putney went to Baggs, while Harvey Logan
(using the name Harvey Ray) and Indian Billy rode to
Dripping Rock in northwestern Colorado.

Putney ran into Flat Nose and Longabaugh at Baggs, and
they drifted into Montana to rob a train. Sixshooter Bill
Smith and a deputy overtook them in camp shortly after
they got inside the Montana state line and before they got
any trains robbed. In the gun battle, Flat Nose was shot in
the arm. The posse had foresightedly collected the horses
before mixing it up with the bad men, so the fellows surrendered. Charged with the Belle Fourche robbery, all three
were taken to Deadwood and lodged in jail. The Deadwood
jail was more secure than the one at Belle Fourche, and
the lawmen intended to hang onto the boys. Although Flat
Nose and Longabaugh had nothing to do with the bank
robbery, they had to stay in jail and await trial.

Also in the jail at Deadwood, besides Peep O'Day, were
two others, a Negro called Speck, who had killed a woman,

and a simple sort of fellow who seemed to have the run of the jail. The boys persuaded this simpleton, while outside the cell, to throw a lever on the lock which had to be tripped from inside the cell to put the lock back into operation. This was a safety measure in case a mob tried to take a prisoner out of custody.

The jailer had been warned to be on his guard all the time, and he looked the situation over carefully, but it looked all right. Longabaugh was sitting on an overturned bucket reading a newspaper, and the rest of the prisoners were near the rear of the cell. As soon as the jailer opened the door and stepped in to trip the lock, Longabaugh hurled himself on the man, throwing him to the floor and knocking the wind out of him.

Flat Nose grabbed the jailer's gun and shot once, and O'Day and Putney got scared, which dulled the edge of their decision. After locking the jailer's wife in the cell with him, to keep her from turning in the alarm, they took off. O'Day and Putney were picked up almost immediately, but the rest were made of sterner stuff.

Flat Nose, Longabaugh and Speck came to a rancher's house where they stole a pair of big, awkward Clydesdale mares that couldn't strike a lope—all they could do was trot. Just at dark, after riding a couple of hours with no saddles and only the blind work-bridles, they came to a bridge guarded by a sheriff's posse. There was nothing to do but trot right onto the bridge, and that is what they did, so boldly that the posse thought it must be the farmer and his hired man with the farmer's son behind him on the mare. Speck was a small man and was riding behind Longabaugh.

The mares gave out that night, not being bred for covering territory, and the three walked for a while. Finally they came to a pasture with some horses grazing inside the fence. These they caught and, mounting up, decided to separate, Longabaugh going north, and the others west.

Longabaugh went down to a little ranch where a fellow owned a race mare and race saddle, both handily kept in the barn. Of course, Longabaugh didn't know this until he got to snooping around, but he took advantage of the opportunity.

The saddle left much to be desired, but up to that time he had been riding bareback, and he wasn't in a position to complain. The mare was just what he needed, and he planned to make tracks.

The mare held out two nights, until they came to the 101 Ranch. Tying her to a fence post, Longabaugh crawled a quarter of a mile across a pasture into a barn and stole a big, black horse and a good saddle. There was a Winchester in the scabbard on the saddle, and a box of shells in the saddle pocket. This fixed him up in first-class shape and he, knowing that the owner would take a limited view of his appropriation of the property, lit a shuck for Hole-in-the-Wall.

Thermopolis, Wyoming, just a camp at that time, saw Longabaugh briefly when he stopped in there to pick up a fresh horse before going on to meet Curry (Logan), Indian Billy and possibly Speck at Powder Springs.

In Vernal, Utah, they outfitted with a wagon and team for a camp outfit. This was luxury. They had been traveling light up to now, without even a packhorse, living off the country and sleeping by small campfires.

Speck took over the cooking and driving the wagon, and the outfit moved through the country posing as cattle buyers, a favorite ruse for the Wild Bunch. They landed at the Roost in the fall, and Flat Nose met them there. After an uneventful winter, the boys pulled out in the spring, leaving Speck and the wagon and saying they would be back for him. He waited and waited for them before finally moving on out of the country, no one knows where.

One of the reasons they didn't return was that shortly after leaving the Roost, they ran into a posse. Dropping down into the canyons leading to the Green River, they crossed to the north side, but couldn't find any trails out. They cached their saddles after turning the horses loose on the river bottom and walked out, scaling ledges where horses could not have been taken. When they had walked to the town of Green River, Kid Curry, Longabaugh and Flat Nose caught a freight train and went to Elko, Nevada, where they considered themselves safe enough to settle down for a breather. They hired out as horsebreakers, working on different ranches all summer, and when cold weather struck came into Elko to hole up for the winter.

When spring broke, old habits stirred in the three, and they got a camp outfit and went out about twenty miles to a little seep to camp. When it got dark, they came back with gunny sacks over their heads and robbed a gambling house of $3,000, probably figuring that part of it was their own money. They stayed at the camp a few days until things quieted down a little, then rode on.

In Gillette, Wyoming, the law caught up with them, and they were held for Whiskey Bill, the bartender from Elko, to come and identify them. He had a change of heart and sent word: "How the hell could I recognize them when they had gunny sacks over their heads?" They were released.

These boys were really on their toes that spring, and following their travels on a map, you wonder how they could have covered so much ground in such a short time and made themselves so unpopular with the moneyed element. It seems quite possible that some of the robberies that the Wild Bunch got credit for were not of their doing; they all claimed this was so, but this particular trio stayed together and became well enough known to keep track of.

They took a train to Salt Lake City and went from there to Idaho Springs, Wyoming, where they bought (they *must* have been flush!) horses for the Wilcox Siding holdup. Here they were joined by Lonny Logan, Bill Carver and Ben Kilpatrick, who was known as the Tall Texan. Kid Curry (Logan) was the leader again, as he had been in the Belle Fourche robbery.

A new technique entered the Wilcox Siding holdup; in fact two new refinements were introduced here, one was the uncoupling of the engine and express car and moving them away from the rest of the train, a trick which was used again and again in later robberies. The other was gathering all the horses in the area—both range and wild—and driving them to the site of the contemplated holdup just before the robbery and turning them loose. The robbers then rode unshod horses; thus the tracks were confused beyond all chance of pursuit. This was used on this one job, only.

When the train pulled along the eastward siding at Milepost 609, forty-three miles west of Laramie, roughly halfway between Medicine Bow and Rock River, two men rose

out of the brush and, uncoupling the baggage car, ordered
the engineer to move ahead across the bridge onto the siding. There the safe in the baggage car was blown and $8,000,
besides a big consignment of $20 unsigned notes for the
bank at Portland, were sacked and carried away.

The loot was split as soon as they returned to the grove
of trees where Ben Beeson was holding the horses, and the
boys took off in all directions.

Most of the gang went north from the Wilcox holdup,
and the posse managed to unravel the tracks well enough to
follow Longabaugh, Harvey Logan and Flat Nose George
to a camp in a dugout where they were eating dinner. During the fight, Harvey Logan shot and killed Sheriff Joe
Hazen of Converse County. The posse withdrew, but took
all the horses with them.

The three walked about thirty miles to Bill Hill's ranch
on Powder River (on the Red Fork) and there took his
horses to hit out for the Big Horn Mountains. Harvey Logan, being the "hot" one of the group, hit south toward the
Roost, staying overnight in the cow camp of Ballard Brothers in the Book Cliffs above Thompson. Major A. P. Ballard
wrote me from England, in a letter dated February 29, 1948:

> I was alone in my camp many miles south of the holdup
> when one night a tall, good-looking man rode up and
> asked for shoes for his horse, which I was able to supply.
> This turned out to be Orion Curry, and he gave me, upon
> leaving, an unsigned $20 bill, thus establishing his identity
> with the holdup. All of these men got away to Butch
> Cassidy's stronghold at Robbers Roost . . .

Longabaugh and Flat Nose were just one jump ahead of
the law, and it was taxing them to lay down a tangled
trail. They crossed the Big Horn River at the mouth of
Owl Creek, toward the Sawtooth Range, in the day time so
that everyone could see them and tell the posse "They went
thataway." After dark they doubled back and crossed about
ten miles above the mouth of Owl Creek, going into the Big
Horn Mountains again. There they hid in the timber until
fall, waiting for the hue and cry to die down a little.

When they emerged, Longabaugh turned toward Montana, but Flat Nose stopped off for a while on Hill Creek, just over the Colorado border from Utah, on the north side of the Book Cliffs.

Flat Nose always liked Hill Creek, coming back to that area again and again, until this last time. The winter of 1899-1900 he spent in a cave in Rattlesnake Canyon (together with a good share of robbery loot, it is said) above Green River, Utah, and on the east side of the river. This was below Florence Creek.

Tom Dilly had just bought the Jim McPherson cattle, and he and Billy Rose were gathering them. Flat Nose spent the winter helping them, dropping back to pick up his camp before helping them cross their herd at the mouth of the canyon. Tom Dilly was planning to take the cattle to Range Valley and start an outfit of his own, and had been holding them along the river in the canyon near the mouth of Rattlesnake that bears Flat Nose's name to this day.

Flat Nose stayed in the cave all night, but when he picked up the camp the next morning he didn't take all his belongings, because he had only one packhorse. He left a big Dutch oven, one used only in permanent camps and not carried in light outfits where a smaller one would serve the purpose. Forty years later, Budge (Ray) Wilcox, son-in-law of Jim McPherson, found the old camp with the Dutch oven still sitting where Flat Nose had left it. Budge lifted the lid, and the few biscuits left over from Flat Nose's breakfast looked just as good as ever. Budge tried to pick one up to taste it, but it fell to dust at a touch. Budge still has the Dutch oven.

This was forty years later than the morning Flat Nose threw on his pack and drifted down the canyon, arriving early in the afternoon. The cattle were bunched, and he and Dilly headed the lead into the river, with Billy Rose to bring up the drag. The Green was high, and the cows didn't take it very well, so they were all the rest of the day fighting them across.

At sundown, Flat Nose looked around for his packhorse, but it had disappeared. He followed the packhorse's tracks almost to his winter camp before catching it. Night caught him before he got back to the river. The cattle had gone up the Golden Stairs onto Range Valley Mountain, with Dilly and Rose and their camp and extra saddle horses following them.

When he got to the river, Flat Nose crossed and camped. He turned his horses out in the little river-bank meadow, figuring they were too tired to roam far. But in the morning he found they had crossed the river, and the homesick pack-horse had led the two saddle horses back up Rattlesnake, leaving Flat Nose stranded. He couldn't swim, so he set about making a raft to cross the river.

The three men had been pretty busy gathering the cattle, and knew nothing about the killing of Tyler and Jenkins by a band of outlaws just going through the country. The two posses, one under Crip Taylor, and the other under Preece of Vernal, had fallen in behind the cow herd instead of taking the tracks of the killers. Preece had crossed the river at Florence Creek and had come up the west side to head off Dilly and Flat Nose, whom they were after on general principles, using the Tyler-Jenkins murder as an excuse. Taylor's posse saw Flat Nose first.

Flat Nose, busy lashing a raft together, looked up at a hail from across the river and was ordered to surrender. (The posse perhaps believed him to be Dilly since he was quite a distance from them.) Flat Nose started to run back to camp, and Doc King, foreman for the Webster City Cattle Company, shot at him, making a freak hit—as it was several hundred yards. Flat Nose made it to camp, and got his gun, then crawled up in the rocks and forted up. Here he died from Doc's bullet, leaning against a rock with his gun across his lap.

Preece's posse came down to the top of the Golden Stairs where they could see Flat Nose, but the posse didn't know he was dead. After watching him for a while, they finally approached him and discovered he had robbed his last train. His body was taken to Thompson for a coroner's inquest and was buried there. His father came from Shadron, Nebraska, several months later, disinterred the body and took it back to Nebraska for final burial.

Although Flat Nose was now out of the picture, Longabaugh and Logan were still very much at large. Harvey Logan had remembered some unfinished business in Montana; he returned there soon after the Wilcox Siding holdup and shot Winters in cold blood, then rode south, catching up with Longabaugh in New Mexico.

The Wild Bunch was robbing right and left now, mostly trains, until the situation got so hot they had to pull out for South America. Just before they left, they all gathered at Fort Worth, Texas, for a final celebration, where they bought derby hats and had a group picture taken. It is said that Butch Cassidy sent this picture back to the bank at Winnemucca which they had just robbed, together with a note of appreciation for the bank's contribution.

The Pinkerton Detective Agency had been following Butch for a few years at the behest of the railroads, but either he was unaware of their interest or else he just ignored it. They were not so well organized in the West at that time and probably were not as lucky in their choice of personnel as they might have been. At any rate, they turned their attention to hunting down the lesser members of the "Train Robbing Syndicate" as the Wild Bunch had begun calling themselves.

According to an article by Arthur Chapman in the April, 1930, issue of the *Elks Magazine*, Harvey Logan met his end thus:

> The chief efforts of the authorities were centered on the capture of Harvey Logan, the tiger of the Hole-in-the-Wall gang. Posters offering heavy rewards for him dead or alive stared at Logan from every town and hamlet in the West. He turned south and narrowly escaped capture at Nashville, Tenn. The unsigned currency again! It was a signpost, calling attention to his whereabouts. Still, when a man needed money, he had to take a desperate chance. Logan passed out some bills in a Knoxville saloon. Police soon stood at the front and back doors. Logan shot and dangerously wounded two policemen and a bartender and escaped by jumping thirty feet into a railroad cut. Two days later he was caught, owing to injuries received in the leap. He was given ten sentences aggregating 130 years. While awaiting removal to the penitentiary, Logan caught the warden of the Knox County jail in a noose made of broom wire. Drawing the jailer to his cell door, Logan reached through and took the keys from his pocket and escaped.
>
> After that it was back to the West, with the intention of

taking up the old trade of train robbery. But Cassidys and Longabaughs were not to be found everywhere. The old-time finesse was lacking in the first holdup on the Denver and Rio Grande at Parachute, Colorado. The train was held up by three robbers, who had been loitering in the vicinity for some time. One of them gave the name of Tap Duncan.

After the holdup, a posse was quickly on the trail—so quickly that the robbers soon found themselves at bay in a mountain gulch. The bandit who called himself Tap Duncan was wounded. He tried to get on his horse and failed. Then the other train robbers tried to help him on one of their mounts.

"It's no use, boys—I'm done. Go on without me," the wounded robber was heard to say.

As his companions left at a gallop, the bandit sank behind a rock and opened fire on the sheriff's posse. It was just a bluff to save his pals, but it worked. The posse moved forward slowly, keeping up a heavy fire. There came the sound of a single revolver shot from behind the rock. He had shot himself when he saw that the game was up. Sheriffs and detectives all over the country breathed easier when it was learned later that the so-called Tap Duncan was really Harvey Logan.

Logan was killed June 7, 1904. . . .

Two events in 1970 focused attention on Wild Bunch history: The movie, *Butch Cassidy and the Sundance Kid* swept the country, and Harry Longabaugh, Jr., came into Ogden, Utah, doing research on his suddenly illustrious father. The movie, a fabulous spoof on Westerns, was out of this world as entertainment, but it made no pretensions to documentary status.

Longabaugh, however, was a different proposition; he claimed to be the legitimate son of the Sundance Kid, and said he had proof. While he didn't produce the proof, at least to me, he did have some information not generally known, and which later research in the proper quarters revealed to be quite accurate.

His speech at the Weber County Library at Ogden, Utah,

on June 25, 1970, throws a different light on the demise of Harvey Logan—or at least on the identification of the outlaw of the Parachute, Colorado, train robbery:

> Ever since I met Harvey Logan, I have tried to find out how he was identified (following the Parachute robbery), who identified him, what methods were used and so forth. For 45 years these questions have bugged me. . . . Well, I finally found out how they identified him.
>
> They found a paper in his pocket bearing the name of Ora Kilpatrick, a resident of Knickerbocker, Texas. Ora was the sister of this Ben Kilpatrick, the Tall Texan. So they wrote her a letter giving her his description and she wrote back saying that from this description she assumed it to be this Tap Duncan, one of Harvey Logan's aliases.
>
> And the body laid there for three weeks, unburied, while a man named McAllister tried to identify him by phrenology, a pseudo-science that has been debunked for many years. Well, apparently they got a little greedy for the reward money on him, because they buried him as Tap Duncan.
>
> But the Union Pacific Railroad, Federal Government and others insisted it was not Harvey Logan, alias Tap Duncan. Dug him up on July 16, but the body was decomposed (I'll *bet* it was!) so bad they couldn't identify it.

Longabaugh identifies this man as Matt Brady, but in all probability it was Lonny Logan, as he seems to have dropped out of the picture.

Back in 1897, Kid Curry (Harvey Logan) joined Butch Cassidy and Elzy Lay at the WS cattle ranch at Alma, and helped make a crew there. He took the name of Tom Capehart, and was with Lay and Sam Ketchum at the Colorado Southern train robbery at Folsom. For some reason, he was never identified as one of the outlaws on that job, and he stayed around the WS for a few months after Butch left there, following Lay's trial and imprisonment.

He and Butch Cassidy picked up the Folsom loot and then worked north, where they, together with Harry Longabaugh, robbed the train at Wagner, Montana.

Soon after that he went to Seattle, Washington, where he joined a sailing ship and rode it as far as Valparaiso, Chile, where he jumped ship. There is no doubt he and Butch had made a plan to meet in South America, since he joined them at Chubut. In all probability, he was disappointed when he found Sundance with Butch, since they had never been particularly close before; it is likely that Logan thought that, with Elzy Lay behind bars, he was in the best position to "side" the leader of the Wild Bunch, even in exile, and when he found this was not so, he returned to the United States.

He was involved in the Parachute robbery in 1904, but he was not killed there, but drifted back to New Mexico where he was working in the Alma district when Lay was pardoned from the New Mexico Territorial Prison on January 10, 1906.

There is no doubt that Lay (being watched too closely to go himself) sent Logan to South America to collect his share of the Folsom train robbery. Logan helped Butch rob the bank in Mercedes Province, San Luis, Argentine, to procure the money to bring back to Lay. Butch had invested his money in the ranch at Chubut, and when he needed a large sum of money in a hurry, he knew where to get it—at a bank.

After bringing the money back to Lay, he worked in the United States for a while, then returned to South America. There, according to a letter in 1970 from Frank O'Grady in Ireland to Mrs. Lula Parker Betenson, Butch Cassidy's sister, Logan was killed by a wild mule in 1909.

Thus ended the Curry saga—in violence, with John shot down by a rancher in Montana, Harvey Logan killed by a wild mule in South America and Lonny probably buried on a sidehill in Colorado. Their uncle, Flat Nose George, the "Fagin of the West," as he has been called, taught his pupils all too well the crooked trails of the Western Hemisphere, but he failed to point out that he who lives by the gun will, in most cases, die by it.

Our next man, Bob Ricker, also upholds that general truth.

SOME OTHERS,
INCLUDING
GRIMES & RICKER

The Wild Bunch, as they have come to be called since their era has passed, numbered about twenty or, at most, twenty-five men. But there were never more than five or six on any one job, be it bank robbing or stealing a bunch of cattle. They were a loosely knit bunch, having no recognized leader but drifting around by twos or threes.

Butch Cassidy and Elzy Lay rode stirrup to stirrup, as did Grimes and Bob Ricker; while Indian Ed, Silver Tip and Blue John formed a group, and Flat Nose George always led the Curry boys. Mostly, however, these men drifted about in small groups or rode the long trails alone, whichever suited their fancies at the moment.

While Jack Moore was at the Roost, there would sometimes be as high as fifteen men there, men who had ridden in singly or in groups of two or three during the fall or winter and who stayed all winter and rode out in the spring in the same way.

Probably some of these fellows met the man they usually associated with after they came to the area, but when a

couple of men came into the country, they, being the strangers, naturally paired off, and people came to think of them
as having come into the country together.

This is the case with the saddle bum, Porter. He probably
didn't come into the country with Gunplay Maxwell, but
the first anyone remembers of him, he was with Maxwell
butchering beef to feed the crew of men mining at Bromide
Basin in the Henry Mountains. Maxwell claimed Porter
was killed in the Springville bank robbery, and since he
didn't show up after that, it was probably true.

Another man not connected with these two in any way,
but of some importance because he had enough personality
to leave an impression, was Dan Parker, brother of Butch
Cassidy. He wasn't riding with Butch at the time when
most of the stories told about him occurred, since Butch
was in Wyoming, but he later joined his brother and the
rest of the Wild Bunch. He helped Joe Walker gather and
load out a bunch of cows at Woodside, and seemed to be
available here and there from time to time. He rode either
with the outlaws or the stockmen, the line was too fine for
anyone to quibble about. Company on the lonely ranches was
too precious to foster any moral wrangles.

Dan Parker (or Joe Simms, or Kid Jackson, or Billy the
Kid) had a very noticeable identification mark, he had lost
two fingers off his right hand. His brother was cutting willows for firewood with a hatchet while Dan pushed them
up on the chopping block. He pushed too far once, and lost
most of his second and third fingers.

He drifted into the La Sal-Blue Mountain country,
punching cows, herding sheep or whatever work he could
get to do, holding no particular loyalty to any outfit. He was
always ready to move on, and the last time he did he left
in the night and never went back, having perpetrated one
of those practical jokes that his kind of rough rider found
irresistible.

The *Kansas City Star* had brought out an article on the
outlaws of southwestern Colorado and eastern Utah, and
claimed that their main stopping place was the Carlisle
Ranch on the Blue Mountains, near where Monticello, Utah,
was later settled. Carlisle took exception to this, being the

head of a cattle and sheep outfit owned by wealthy English-
men and strictly honest. He decided to go to Kansas City
and straighten things out, taking his foreman, Len Scott,
along for a witness.

This left the outfit pretty much in the hands of the men,
one sheep outfit in Dry Valley being left under the doubtful
protection of Kid Jackson as Dan Parker was known there.

When Scott returned, scattered around the saddle shed
and granary was a substantial number of pelts from sheep
belonging to Goodman, a rival neighbor. Scott was thankful
he had made it back before Goodman, who cherished no
love for him, had found them and taken action on the theft
by having somebody arrested. In fact, Scott himself toyed
with the idea of calling in the law.

"You didn't eat that many mutton while we were gone?"
he asked Parker, trying to find out how the pelts came to
be there.

"Sure," Dan grinned. "No reason to be too saving; there
was plenty more where those came from."

"I ought to have you arrested," threatened Scott.

"Go ahead. I'll swear I don't know anything about them.
And *you* try to explain them away to Goodman. He'd sure
like to have a chance like this at you."

That made painful sense, but the Carlisle outfit was still
stuck with the hides, and Scott wanted to make things
right. But he didn't know exactly how to go about it so he
took the pelts to Monticello and stored them in an old building—one of the first buildings put up there—while he figured out something to do with them.

A few nights later, Scott and one of the Goodman men
were getting ready to go to a dance, and Goodman's man
wanted to use the old cabin to change clothes in, as they
had done in the past. Because he was half drunk, Scott
forgot about the hides until the two men were right in the
door.

Although the other fellow wasn't in any better shape
than Scott, he saw the hides first thing and, dance forgotten, insisted on loading them on a mule to take to Goodman
for evidence to present to the sheriff, since the cabin belonged to the Carlisle outfit. Scott, sobered considerably,

tried to talk him out of it, but the fellow was mad and packed up his mule.

It was pretty late in the evening by that time. Parker learned somehow what was going on and hung around the edges to see what was going to happen, and also to protect his own interests. He didn't want to be brought to the attention of the sheriff. He couldn't stand too much scrutiny, but things were too interesting to leave just yet. He followed the two fellows as they wrangled, and Scott finally persuaded the man to stop by the White House, Carlisle's home ranch, and have another drink.

Kid saw the opportunity for a colossal joke, and he couldn't resist. While the two were in the house, he hustled around and gathered up some Carlisle pelts, unpacked the mule and replaced the Goodman hides with those from his own outfit, tying them on as nearly as he could like the original pack.

The Goodman man came out in a little while and went on to Goodman's ranch, leading the mule and congratulating himself on having enough evidence to "make good Indians" of that Carlisle outfit for a good long time to come. He pulled into the Goodman ranch toward morning, got Goodman out of bed, telling him to come down with a lantern and see what he had.

"Why didn't you just leave them there and go get the sheriff?" Goodman wanted to know.

"You know that outfit! If I had left those pelts one minute, there wouldn't have been any evidence, and you know it."

Goodman agreed with that.

"Besides, Scott admitted it, and with the pelts as evidence, you have a good case. I think probably they will be down here today to settle with you for the sheep rather than let it get to the sheriff."

By this time they had the mule unpacked and had laid the hides out in the lantern light. Goodman examined one hide, then with an exclamation quickly turned the beams of the lantern on the others.

"You fool!" he said. "These pelts, every one, belong to Carlisle. You better get them right back up there before the sheriff *does* come down here. And you haven't got too much of the night left to do it in, either." And Goodman went swearing back to bed.

Far away by this time, Parker was riding for new territory, laughing as he went.

Another man whose career was brief but eventful in the country was Fred Carter, a fine rider and horseman, who hired out to break a bunch of colts for the Taylor family on the La Sal Mountains. The Taylors didn't have a horse pasture, just rounded up the horses and drove them in, where Carter was supposed to break them to the saddle, hobbling them out at night to graze.

The horses kept getting away from Carter, and the Taylors would ride out from Moab and run in another few head. Carter would get that bunch sacked out pretty well, and ridden a few times, when they would get away, too. The Taylors weren't too concerned; after all he was knocking the rough off quite a bunch of colts, and they were right there on the range somewhere. And they were, too, until one day the horsebreaker and a friend of his who had just showed up left, driving a considerable bunch of horses belonging not only to the Taylors but also to the Wilcox and Larsen families, everybody's that were handy.

A posse followed them a day or two later across the Dolores River, which was in flood. Swimming the river, even as the thieves had done, the posse followed a while longer, but finally gave up and went back home.

Budge Wilcox, son of one of the losers, told this story many years later:

"Myrup and Wim Thompson had a couple of their sheep herds mix on the Book Cliff range one summer, and Dad and I rode up while they were waiting in the corral to get them separated.

"Dad and this herder of Myrup's—Carter, or Mitchell as he was now known—sort of snarled at each other at first, but finally got to talking. Dad told him that some of those horses he had driven out of the country belonged to him, but Carter didn't seem too worried about it. Horses had been plentiful fifty years before, and ownership was apt to change suddenly on quite a bunch. Besides, it had been too long ago to do anything about it now, so Dad got over feeling sore.

"Carter—or Mitchell—went from the Myrup sheep outfit over to the Henry Mountains, where his horses got locoed at the head of Butler Canyon near Granite. He had camped there for the winter, and when he got the team up in the spring and hooked them to the wagon, the horses had a fit and tore up his outfit. That was the last we heard of him."

Three other outlaws, who might have been minor members of the Wild Bunch at one time or another, but whose names were not learned, came through the country about the turn of the century. Bill Tomlinson was carrying the mail on horseback to Hanksville from Green River. One trip he saw, at a little distance east of the trail, a herd of horses and three riders aiming for Temple Mountain and points west, their route shaping up to a meeting with him down the trail a mile or so. He noticed when he speeded up that they slowed down, showing a definite reluctance to have him get too close. Just as he was getting really curious, they dropped into a swale on the far side of a ridge from him. When he got to the rim of the valley, where he could see them again, they had really whipped up and had the horses across the trail and a couple of hundred yards up the draw, still traveling at a pretty good clip. Bill started to follow and one of the fellows rode back.

"You want something?" the fellow inquired when they met.

"Not too much," Bill remarked, "but that bald-faced mare in the lead there looks a lot like one of mine."

"Couldn't be," the fellow said. "We bought all these horses in Moab."

Bill could see there wasn't any profit in crowding the situation, since his duty was to the mail on the packhorse. He went on to Hanksville and when he returned to Green River the next day reported to Harry Farrer what he had seen. Farrer was deputy sheriff, and the Farrers owned a good many horses, too.

Tom, Harry's brother, happened to be in Salina, Utah,

and Harry wired him to ride up Salina Canyon to meet the outfit and look it over. Tom threw on his saddle and did so, riding past the horses, never letting on that he was looking them over, but marking the number of ̅I ̅2̅ (Bar 12) horses in the bunch belonging to him and his brother. He had the sheriff pick the thieves up and land them in the Salina jail.

The jail didn't look very secure to the horsethieves, and they planned to break out as soon as it got dark. Thinking they had better start work on the wall early enough to dig out enough bricks to get away, they started about noon to dig the mortar out and loosen the bricks.

Much to their amazement, the whole wall of the jail fell in, and there was nothing left for them to do but make a break for it. One fellow ran to a ranch, where he stole a team of little black horses belonging to Tom Baker and left the country with the sheriff hot on his trail. They made a run across the San Rafael Desert and crossed the Green and Colorado Rivers, but when they got to the Dolores, there had been a big storm above and the river was raging, bank full. The outlaw piled in and swam across. As he was going up the other bank, the posse rode up to the river. They yelled for him to halt, but he just tendered them a derisive gesture and rode off. They shot a few times but didn't hit him. The horses were never recovered.

Of the other two horsethieves, one got away without the law ever knowing quite where he went, but the remaining one was caught. Bill Tomlinson was called as a witness and made a trip to Manti, where he met the sheriff on the street. The sheriff pointed across the street and asked Bill if he had ever seen that fellow before. Bill, expecting to see an acquaintance, looked carefully, then had to admit that he didn't believe he ever had. There was never a trial, Bill had failed to identify the criminal. When told of this, Bill took his bald-faced mare and went home, the Farrers took their horses and did likewise, and no one knew what became of the outlaw and the few horses he still had.

George Range (sometimes known as Range or Raines Lee—supposed to be a brother of John D. Lee, the Mormon leader who was executed for the Mountain Meadows Mas-

sacre) had a brief life of outlawry. He stopped at a sheep
camp on the Henry Mountains, where a Mexican by the
name of Beshago was staying alone. The two got into a
card game in the evening, and some trouble developed.
Range shot the Mexican, took all the horses belonging to
the sheep outfit and left the country for a time.

The Mexican wasn't killed, however. The bullet had gone
through his mouth, breaking his jaw. After a while he came
to and thought he'd better go for help. He walked into
Hanksville, some 25 miles, and stayed there with Goulds,
until his brother came and got him.

George Range returned to the country after a few years,
and was called to Loa to testify at a trial as to Silvertip's
good character. He came back through Fruita from Loa
with a team and light wagon, but was not seen after that.

Just a few years ago a skeleton was found at a little seep
back in the wilds from Fruita, and oldtimers speculated
that the Mexican had followed Range back into the country,
and, seeing a good opportunity, had killed him and then
took the wagon toward Mexico.

While these men were undoubtedly part of the Wild
Bunch, most of them were on the outer fringe, and it is
doubtful that they ever spent much time with Butch Cassidy
and his inner circle. However, Grimes and Ricker were more
active members and camped at the Roost for months at a
time, usually with Butch.

Grimes seems to have drifted into the Roost alone and to
have put in with Ricker after he got there. He'd had a fight
with a sheepherder at the Ireland Ranch, near Salina, and
figuring that the sheepman had been killed, made a run for
the Roost. But he might have known a sheepherder can't be
killed honorably, and the fellow was looking for Grimes to
prefer charges of a lesser import than murder. This indi-
cated hunting cover, and Grimes did.

He spent the winter at the Roost. Then, thinking it the
best policy to re-locate in the opposite direction, rode out
toward Douglas Creek and the Webster City Cattle Company on the north slope of the Book Cliffs. Jim Rector was
running the outfit, just before Bart Owens took it over.

There, Grimes got into some kind of fight with one of the cowboys, a fellow by the name of Billings, and was more successful than he had been with the sheepherder.

Grimes rode Old Headlight back to the Roost. Headlight was a big brown horse with a round white spot on his forehead, weighed well over a thousand pounds and was "all horse." This was pretty big for those times, most of the saddle horses weighed about 850 to 1,000 pounds, with the biggest horses coming from the north and the smaller, Spanish-type ponies, coming up from Arizona and New Mexico.

Headlight may have been a good horse, but he kicked Sunday, the little dog that Neil Hanks had at the Roost, and broke the puppy's leg. Neil splinted Sunday's leg and carried him in a nosebag on the saddle until the bone knitted again. The men couldn't forget how the accident happened, and they had no use for Headlight. This didn't alter the fact that Headlight was a fine horse, good enough to be in the string when Jack Moore, Grimes and Bob Ricker stole the Starr-Thompson cattle on the Henry Mountains.

Starting early in the spring, before the first roundup of the season, the three carried out a carefully planned campaign. Mindful of what tracks could reveal, especially those impressed into spring mud like plaster casts, the three gathered small bunches of cattle from which they cut out a few selected animals, dry cows and steers—strong, thrifty and wild. Pushing these by tens and fifteens down Poison Spring Canyon, they left little indication on the range of the three hundred head of stock, which was about what they figured they could handle.

Starting at Poison Spring itself one May morning, they rode down the canyon, spooking the cattle ahead of them. Crossing the Dirty Devil at the mouth of the canyon, they eased the cattle up onto the bench at the mouth of Hatchie Canyon. This was the first time the herd had been all rounded up into one bunch.

Jack rode through it several times, cutting back a few head of weak stock. These, he and Grimes shoved back down to the Dirty Devil, while Ricker hazed the trimmed herd up Hatchie Canyon. When the two overtook the trail herd, they had picked up the packs and extra saddle horse, and Jack had changed his saddle from Turk to one of the lesser mounts in his string.

After a hasty lunch near a water tank in a little side canyon, Jack rode on through the cattle to hold back the leaders until the other two could haze up the drag. Thrown into a compact herd once more, the cattle calmed and became a mobile unit. Those few free spirits, planning escape, soon found the way blocked by a competent horseman, wielding a snapping rope.

By the time the herd siphoned through Sunset Pass and spread out on Waterhole Flats, it was shaping up to the satisfaction of the riders. Since there was water everywhere on the rocks from a recent rain, it was decided to hold over a day to rest and fill the herd up for the hard trip ahead. There would be no forage down the Spanish Trail to the river, not much but salt grass on Spanish Bottom, and nothing on the farther side until they climbed out near the Abajo Mountains.

Camp was thrown off the packs in Sunset Pass to hold the back trail. There wasn't much of any place the cattle could stray to overnight, so the three men held until dark, bedding the cattle skillfully, then returning to camp for a late supper and a short night's rest.

Catching the more restive leaders the next morning just at daylight, they had the cattle rounded up and grazing by mid-morning. A whole tedious day stretched ahead of the men. One rider could dayherd, and the three riders leaned on their saddlehorns and wondered how to kill the day.

"Tell you what," Jack Moore said, "let's a couple of us ride down and look off the ledge into Cataract Canyon."

"Go ahead," Ricker spoke up. "I'll dayherd."

Jack and Grimes turned their horses south to where the narrow gash of the Colorado a mile or so away sliced off the edge of the flats. It was some time before they got close enough to distinguish the canyon, so narrow and hidden it was.

"Looks like a man could ride right across here onto that point," Grimes commented.

"There's a hell of a sight of country between here and

that point," Jack answered. "But sure would be handy. We're not across the Colorado, yet."

"Or out the other side," Grimes agreed.

Far below them, down a slightly undercut cliff, ran the Colorado River, looking thin and puny in the depths of the narrow gorge. Across it the broken country rose in mesas slashed by rocky canyons up to where the cedared flanks of the Abajo seemed to smooth the gouged earth.

Jack sat down on the ledge, with his feet hanging over the sheer drop. This Grimes could not do; in fact he could only get close enough to stretch and peer over the edge.

"Sure is deep," he ventured.

"Sure is." Jack was packing his pipe. He scratched a match on the rock at his side, and held it to his pipe. "They say the Milk River in Montana is a mile wide and an inch deep. I think of that, backwards, whenever I look down this canyon." He flipped the match out into nothingness. "Them white spots are rapids, plenty of 'em."

Grimes watched the river for a few moments, counting eleven separate rapids from where they stood. "Anyone ever go down that part of the river in a boat?" he asked.

"Oh, sure. Probably more than got credit for it. Well, let's amble back and eat, and relieve Bob."

Next morning the cattle were crowded down the Spanish steps and the rough trail onto Spanish Bottom. The riders let the cattle drop back after watering, then rode down the bank to pick a crossing. They watched the muddy waters, swirling in treacherous undercurrents, rolling and turning heavily.

"Now, what the hell do we do?" Grimes stepped back to higher ground, out of the mud near the lapping water's edge as his horse finished drinking.

"Go back, I guess." Moore answered gloomily.

"Like hell we will." Ricker spoke decisively. "You desert rats scared of a little water?"

"Me—I am." Moore looked at the far bank. "We got to cross damn near straight over, the river has come up over that long gravel bar I remembered, and that cut bank runs a half mile farther up the stream than I recall it."

"But when they hit that bar you talk about, they'll be

through the main current and will even wade upstream if
they have to," Ricker argued. The water did seem to flatten
out on the far side.

"But the ones that don't quite make it—goodbye! If a
cow—or man—falls only just a little short, that's all,
brother! That's plumb all!"

Next morning the river had dropped a good eighteen
inches; things looked brighter. The upper edge of the gravel
bar showed for a few yards, but the rocks still struck
solidly down into the river at the lower end.

They threw the bunch together and headed for the crossing. Moore was on Turk, Grimes on Headlight and Ricker
on a big sorrel, all grain-fed and hardened by just enough
riding, but saved for this job.

All went well as they hazed the herd pretty well into the
stream. There, the bunch balked. The sun, shining on the
water, blinded the cows, and they wouldn't take the deep
water. The three cowboys dropped back, and with swinging ropes and wild yells, pushed the herd forward, forcing
the leaders into swimming water.

Blinded by the sun reflected on the water, deafened by
the roaring and splashing, forced into this dangerous un-
familiar element by the pressure of the bodies behind
them, the leaders bolted, heading downstream. The men
flailed their strong horses up along the downstream side of
the bunch of swimming cattle, trying to swing them up
into the current. Suddenly the herd whipped into a mill,
crowding closer until the inside circles were trampled under.
The men were able to cut off and head only about ninety of
the strongest outside cattle into the bank. The rest were
swept downstream, the heavy, silt-laden water rolling them
end over end.

In fifteen minutes it was finished, and the three men on
trembling, winded horses, huddled together on the bank and
watched the last of the main herd, swimming feebly, carried helplessly on the crest of the current down the river
and out of sight.

Ricker, after the horses had rested a while, mounted
Headlight and went back for the packs and the other
horses. It was afternoon, no problem with the sun, and the
horses swam across with no trouble.

Next morning the boys started the shrunken herd up the old Spanish trail. Dark hit them shortly after they had made the hardest climb out of the canyon, and they bedded the tired herd for a few hours. Taking advantage of a late moon, they topped out onto Hart Draw just before daybreak and hazed the bunch past Peter's Spring before anyone was around to bother them. It was only a few miles to the Colorado line, but while they were still in Utah they didn't plan to take chances.

Tom Foy was putting up hay at the ranch at Peter's Spring and heard the cattle go past. That day the Indian Creek Cattle Company riders came along, and he told them about the drive. They took the fresh trail and overtook the weary herd in a few miles. Shorty Connel (Bogus Shorty) rode through the cattle, but found nothing belonging to his outfit.

However, when Bogus Shorty returned to the ranch and talked to Foy again, he described the brands, and Foy recognized Wim Thompson's brand. He wrote to Wim and told him about the herd.

Wim got on the job right away and overtook the herd at Telluride, Colorado, where Alex Calhoun had just bought them on a bill of sale signed by Ricker. Wim replevined the cattle, both his and those belonging to Star and Sanford, and sold them again to Calhoun for $14 a head.

After signing the bill of sale, Ricker and Grimes went straight through Utah to Nevada, getting a job with the B. F. Saunders outfit. The law was getting a little narrow-minded about the boys, so they separated, Ricker going to Montana with a cattle drive.

When Ricker didn't return to the Saunders outfit as he expected, Grimes left and went back to Leavenworth, Kansas, where he worked for a while. Then, he traveled on to Wichita, where he married and ran a hotel for several years. A fellow from Moab happened to stay there one time, and Grimes carefully questioned him about Utah.

When his wife died, he returned West, but the old days were gone. No one knew him any more, and he didn't see a familiar face. He drifted on into Nevada, where he dropped out of sight, "maybe down around Pioche."

Although Grimes and Ricker were together a great deal,

it was Ricker that people remembered, and oldtimers recall that he was well-liked and pleasant to be around. He was small, weighed only about 140 pounds, but was a fine athlete. One of the best wrestlers in the state, he could pick up men that weighed 200 pounds, and throw them over his head. He was also one of the best cowboys around, a fine bronc rider and a good horse breaker.

Ricker started west from Kansas, where he had grown up. His first work was on the Pike's Peak road in Colorado. When that was finished, he came to Utah, returning to his first love of riding. He worked for Alfred Starr on the Henry Mountains for a couple of years. He went from there to the H-Bar-T connected on the Blue Mountains at White Canyon. That was the summer before he got into the stealing scrape with the Starr-Thompson cattle. That was his first slip.

On his way back to Nevada from Montana, where he had gone with the Saunders cattle, Ricker ran into Wim Thompson in Salt Lake City. Wim was most cordial. As far as he knew, Ricker had no reason to suspect him, and they had been cow-camp friends for several years. He bought the drinks and suggested they meet that evening down in front of the court house and take in a good show.

Bob said that sounded like a fine idea. As he walked down the street, he grinned. Didn't Wim know that the information passed on when riders met on the back trails was accurate and complete? Bob had known for months that Wim had followed the cattle to Telluride and replevined them, and it was a cinch Wim hadn't forgotten that the bill of sale carried the name of Robert Ricker.

Afraid to try to board the train late that afternoon at the city depot, he walked to Murray where he caught the train for Price. Not seeing any law around when he descended there, he chanced the stage to Ferron, arriving there the next morning.

It was no trick to borrow a horse from a fellow he knew and head for the Roost. He made it fine until he watered his horse in Straight Wash, where, like Jack Moore a few months later, he discovered his error. Sometimes the Straight Wash water was all right; then again, particularly if the horse was warmed up, it would kill him deader than a

Bob Ricker is on the left, Rufe Stoddard in the center, and Al Starr at the right.

—PHOTO COURTESY OF MRS. MART ROBISON, HANKSVILLE, UTAH

wedge. Ricker didn't favor his horse too much, especially when he was in a hurry. The water had done its worst in less than two miles.

When the horse began to stagger and weaken, Bob started to worry. With a good horse under him, he felt he didn't have too much to fear from a posse, but if there was law somewhere between where he stood on a sand bump of the San Rafael Desert and Salt Lake City, he didn't stand a Chinaman's chance without a horse.

Gray light was just topping the eastern rim of the desert as he pulled the saddle off the trembling horse. He tied his lariat around the neck of the animal, and let it out to the length of the rope, where it could feel free to roll and rest, and returned to the saddle. He rolled and lit a smoke, watching the horse in the dim light. He recalled it was now the Fourth of July, but could think of no reason to celebrate.

The light strengthened as Bob flipped his cigarette butt toward a bush, where a bird was sleepily greeting the day. Over on the ridge a coyote bade farewell to the night's hunting and greeted another scorcher of a day on the desert. The horse stretched out on his side and gave a couple of convulsive kicks. Bob walked over to retrieve his rope, knowing before he had moved a step that the horse was dead.

Standing over the carcass, coiling up his rope, Bob weighed his chances. To return to Ferron was unthinkable. It was better than sixty miles, surely, and there was always

The Flat Tops, showing almost the exact route that Bob Ricker walked to the Roost. Note the waves in the blow sand, like those through which he waded.

—PHOTO COURTESY OF PARKER HAMILTON, FLAGSTAFF, ARIZONA

the possibility of a posse. He might walk the forty miles or so into Green River, but where would he be then? He'd better go on to the Roost. It was only about thirty miles, but such miles—uphill most of the way and in the hot, sliding sand of the desert!

Taking off his spurs, Bob buckled them to his belt, and, after stashing his saddle under a serviceberry bush, picked up his rope and turned to leave. He looked with longing at his rifle, but ounces were plenty important right now, and he figured his revolver would have to do. A rifle was handy to move back pursuers, but he didn't plan to linger any the next ten or twelve miles; and if he made it to the Roost, he could get by with a shorter-range gun.

Not many men would have tackled the trip that lay ahead of Bob—thirty miles of desert, rising the first fifteen miles quite abruptly over ridges and swales, with footing every step of the way in the shifting loose sand. He believed the coyote—this July day would be a scorcher, and the only water he would hit would be the wet spot at Sweet Water. As he climbed out of the first draw on his long walk, he concluded wryly that if sunstroke didn't get him, thirst would.

Blazing noon found Bob just topping out on the Sweet Water ridge. He had had a good drink at the hole he had scraped out in the wet sand, but he had been afraid of stiffening up, so he stopped in the shade of a serviceberry bush only long enough for a smoke.

The jaunty swing of his walk had been replaced by a dogged rhythmic slogging that ate away at the sizzling miles. Eyeing his boots, he fully expected to see blue flames playing over them. He wiggled his toes, but he knew better than to take off his boots to see how bad his feet were.

The going was better across the top of North Spring Flats. The sand was firmed by gravel, and the draws were shallow, the ridges low. He winced as he remembered that the last couple of miles lay downhill into the Roost canyon. He rolled a small pebble in his mouth to keep his tongue moist, and left a straight row of tracks until he hit the sand again. He glanced toward Hanksville, thirty miles to his right and murmured, "You people think you are having a hot time over there on this glorious Fourth of July, but I'm having a helluva lot hotter one out on this old desert."

He wondered if he was rambling a little from the heat when this sounded funny to him, and stopped in his tracks to rest his trembling legs and size up the situation. It was only four or five miles to where the trail broke over into the Roost drainage, but between him and the ridge was the fantastically scooped and piled sand of the head of Antelope Valley, almost flat looking, but he knew it was heartbreaking in its pimply hillocks where the grass and small brush had caught the blow-sand. He was sinking to his ankles in the hot sand at every step and had long since decided to ignore his feet.

Raising his bloodshot eyes to the horizon, Bob figured if he could make it to the ridge above the Roost he could coast in, but he knew in his heart he was just lying to himself. Downhill was going to be exquisite torture to his raw feet and aching leg muscles by that time. He smiled grimly as he argued that it would surely be easier to carry his 140 pounds downhill than to drag it upgrade.

The sun was hanging motionless, about halfway down the sky, Bob thought, when he topped the ridge and dropped into the trail from Antelope Valley to the Roost. At least from here on he wouldn't have to pick whether to go right or left or over the top of each of a million sand bumps. He could just stagger down the trail.

Bob never could remember afterward about his trip into the Roost from there. He could recall seeing a small bunch of antelope that spooked off the trail as he met them face to face in a gap of the sand rocks on the ridge. He recalled, too, that somewhere he had lost the pebble he was mouthing, either swallowed it or maybe spat it out and said the hell with it, too tired to stoop over and pick up another one as he slogged along. Just before he lost consciousness and started wandering aimlessly he smelled the bitter sulphur of the Roost. He eagerly drew in a lungful of the smell of wetness.

Dropping down the side wash, he hit wet sand, and believed he could feel the coolness through his blistered feet to the top of his head. Crossing the bunch ground above the

spring, he dropped over the little hill and rounded the turn
into the troughs, where the tinkle of water into the trough
was lost in the splash he made as he flung himself headlong
into the cold wetness.

He drank sparingly, sloshing the water again and again
over his head for the first few minutes. He recalled with
amusement that always before he had turned up his nose
at the bitter Roost water and had ridden up the draw to
the little sweet spring in the side canyon. Today the gypsum
impregnated water, reeking with sulphide, was good enough.

He took his boots off at last, and soaked his raw feet in
the cold water, sitting on the bank behind the trough and
leaning against its comforting wetness. He dozed and wakened for three or four hours until the cold water had taken
some of the fever out of the broken blisters of his mutilated
feet. Washing out his socks, he hobbled barefoot down the
canyon to where he could rest on the dry bank of the canyon
stream. He hung the socks to dry, and when they had dried
late that night, rubbed them soft. It wasn't much, but he
could bear to slip his boots back on early the next morning.

He noted as he left the troughs that night that there
were no riders around to lend a hand corraling some of
the horses whose marks he saw in the mud. No boot tracks
showed at the trough, and he judged by the signs that the
horses watering there were loose, not carrying riders.

Just at dusk a bunch of cattle strung into water. Ricker
heard them at the trough and, peering around the big rock
he was resting against, he picked out a fat calf which he
dropped with his first shot. He stripped out the loin, and
built a fire to roast some chunks of it over the coals. This
was his first meal since leaving Ferron. He skinned out the
hind quarter and hung it on the fence post, dragging the
rest up on the bunch ground where the coyotes would clean
it up to the last morsel before morning.

Bob dropped down the canyon around the turn from the
spring, and climbed up on a narrow shelf. If a posse trailed
him this far, he would have the advantage when daylight
came if they were near. The canyon was narrow, and he
could clean out quite a band with his hand gun before
they could either get away or pot him. He rather hoped a

posse would show up, that would be the easiest way he could think of to get a horse, and he needed a mount. With none of the Bunch around the Roost, he was going to have trouble getting mounted up again.

Sleeping soundly until just before dawn, Bob awoke and pondered the problem he had last thought of—getting a horse. He still had his rope, but he didn't dare make a trap to catch a horse; there was too much danger of losing it. He had shot the calf with his .44, but he didn't know if he could "crease" a horse skillfully enough to knock him down and not put him out of business—but he planned to try it as a last resort.

His thoughts were cut short soon after he had wriggled into his boots and had walked a few steps to make sure he could perambulate again by the measured beat of a band of horses coming down the wash above the spring. He stepped gingerly up to the turn of the canyon to watch for them. It was getting lighter by the minute, and he could see pretty well when the pounding of the horses' hooves crossed the bunch ground and dropped over the hill and around the end of the trough. Just before they came in sight, Bob jumped over to the end of the trough and crouched down. But in his haste, he dropped his lariat. There was nothing to do but wait and hope for a break.

Luck was with him. The bunch of eleven head of horses, intent on quenching their thirst, didn't see him in the dim light, and the last to shove his head in the trough right over Bob was Old Tom, a big brown ⊥ horse. Bob remembered Tom was head-shy, having been beaten over the head as a colt. Any quick move made him dodge and shut his eyes.

Do or die, Bob jumped up beside the old horse, waving his arms. Sure enough, Old Tom forgot to run as the others did and held his head up and away from Bob, shutting his eyes waiting for the blow to descend across his face. Bob locked his arms around the old horse's neck and it was too late for Tom to run, although he tried. Bob set his boot heels grimly and hollered, and Tom finally came to a stop.

It took only a moment for Bob to jerk off his belt and put it around Tom's neck to lead him back to the rope. He fashioned a war bridle and, jumping on the old horse's back, was in business. He had slapped his spurs back on, and he struck them in, loping up the draw after the spooked horses. Sun-up found him just putting up the bars of the corral half a mile above the bunch ground on the north side of the canyon as he looked over his take.

He roped out Coaly, a little black horse, the best in the bunch. Whoever his former owner had been, he now belonged loosely to Jack Moore. Coaly followed the milling horses, spooking and straining against the rope, but in a few minutes Bob had quieted him and walked up to him. He had taken the war bridle off Tom, and now put it on Coaly. The way the little horse was snorting, Bob was glad he had his spurs. Equipped with his trusty gut-hooks, he felt equal to just about anything that wore hair.

Mack, a little bay horse that had been brought into the country with Coaly and always teamed up with him on the range, came out of the bunch to stand by his mate.

Bob considered. Probably he never again would have to go through the grueling experience of the past day or two, but a little insurance wouldn't hurt. He walked up and tied the other end of his rope around Mack's neck, thought a moment, then took out his pocket knife and cut the rope in two. Sure hard on a lasso, but it doubled his chances of hanging onto a mount.

Bob pulled into the ranch of his friend at Ferron the next evening shortly after dark, just to be on the safe side. But no posse had followed him, and he decided that Wim had changed his mind. Paying for the dead horse and buying the saddle, which he had picked up on his way back, he started to leave the country. He left word for Jack Moore that Coaly had led Mack out of the country, but not to tell him that Mack had led Coaly part of the way.

With Mack and Coaly, Ricker went on to Fort Duchesne. Close to the fort a small area of land had been withdrawn from the Indian reservation for the use of white people who were mining gilsonite. Tom Nichols had a saloon on the Strip, and Ricker settled in there, bootlegging liquor to the Indians.

The soldiers at the Fort caught up with him and tossed

him into the pokey. There he stayed for a few days, outwardly resigned, but looking for any chance to make a getaway.

One evening the guard glanced through the barred door and seeing Ricker stretched out on the bed with his boots off, thought it safe enough to enter with the prisoner's supper. He didn't know Ricker. As soon as he was well into the cell, Ricker shot up off the bed, slapped the tray of beans and coffee into the surprised guard's face and ran over him, banging the cell door shut. He ran down the hall, leaped outside and made for the river barefooted.

The soldiers knew he couldn't go far in that rocky country without footgear, so they quickly made up a detail, mounted and took after him. It was getting late in the evening, after sundown, as the soldiers rode toward the saloon, crossing the bridge that concealed Ricker. He peered out through the willows and counted them over, then desperately looked the somewhat bare river bank over for a better hiding place. He knew they would look under that bridge on the way back, that being the only place where a man could hide anywhere close by. Before he could formulate a plan, he heard the soldiers pounding back and, much to his amazement, counted the same number against the sky as they recrossed the bridge toward the fort without stopping.

Waiting only until it was fully dark, Ricker made his way to the saloon, where Tom rustled him a pair of shoes. Tom advised him to go down to the gilsonite mine, where Tom Taylor was foreman, and keep very much out of sight for a few days. Ricker hid in the mine, while the soldiers searched the Strip and beat the boondocks up and down the creek for miles hunting for him.

When the furor had died down a little, Tom Taylor saddled Coaly and brought him and Mack up to the mine late one night. Ricker left for Baggs, Wyoming, where Tom Nichols' brother, Mid Nichols, had a saloon. Ricker still had some of his bootlegging money that he had left with Tom before he was arrested, so he stayed around Baggs celebrating.

One evening Mid bounced him out. He was drunk and

noisy. Going over to one of the other saloons, he got drunker and noisier as the night wore on. Finally the bartender had cleared the place of all but Ricker, and after an hour or so coaxed him outside, also. The bartender was putting things to rights after locking up, when Ricker, discovering that all the rest of the saloons were closed, staggered back and demanded to be let in. The bartender told him to go home and go to bed; he was closed for the night.

Ricker threatened to break the door down.

"Go on! Beat it! If you try to bust that door in, you'll be sorry," the saloon man threatened.

"The hell I will," Ricker blustered. "I'm not the only one; after I get this door kicked in, I'll take care of you."

The saloon-keeper had had a good deal more than enough of Bob, and he grabbed the gun behind the bar and let drive at the splintering door. The shot caught Ricker right in the middle, and he was dead before he hit the sidewalk.

Mid Nichols was called and took care of the burial, for he had known Bob Ricker well. Later that fall he had to do the same thing for Jack Moore—sad endings for cowboys who rode so high and handsome, and it marked the beginning of the end for the Wild Bunch.

Some of them were still around, however. Going back ten years or so, another group who always rode together also had a lively story. Silver Tip, Blue John and Indian Ed Newcomb added their bit to swell the reputation of the Wild Bunch.

Silver Tip was considerably older than the rest of the Robbers Roosters, being about forty or thereabouts in 1890. He had dark brown hair, blue eyes, and always wore a big moustache. His hair around the temples was just turning gray, giving him the name of Silver Tip, especially since he was heavy-shouldered and walked with a roll like a grizzly bear.

According to men who remember him best, his name was Jim Wall.* Names were not very important—even descriptions of men bear the same wording for man after man of that restless fraternity: "Medium-sized and sandy complected." One didn't look at a man too closely, but politely treated the stranger casually.

Now his horse was different—everyone appreciated a good horse, and those men rode the best. Fifty years later some of the oldtimers can describe a horse to the last sad-

---

* Marvel Lay Murdock (Mrs. J. T. Murdock) of Heber City, Utah, remembers him as Bill Wall, and says she visited him once when she was staying with her father, Elzy Lay, in Shoshoni, Wyoming.

dlemark, and these descriptions tally, one with another. They *knew* those horses, horses carried a great deal more personality than the men who rode them.

Silver Tip and ten companions (one a Negro) rode into the country in the fall of 1889 or 1890, landing at the mouth of White Canyon across the Colorado River from Hite. They loafed around all winter, marking time until spring, enjoying the mildness of the weather down in the canyon. They used to watch their horses up on the flats at the head of Farley Canyon or down on the Dorothy Bar, where the feed was good; and they killed a beef of Scorup's, the local cattleman, when the grubstake got short.

Early one morning Al Scorup came upon the camp. A fresh beef hung in a willow tree. The fellows around the fire spoke to him as he rode up and asked him down for a cup of coffee. Al thanked them, got off and accepted the tin cup. Indicating the beef, he asked mildly that they indulge in that only as often as necessary.

"We don't waste none of it, mister," one of the men said, "but you know how it is, a feller has got to eat."

Scorup agreed. There was no need arguing about it, and if he could maintain fairly friendly relations with them, they might have a chance to save a cow or two from the mud of the river, or look after his interests in some other way. They were going to kill what beef they needed, anyway, and it might turn out to be a cheap investment. He caught his packmule, cut off a quarter of the beef, and loaded it onto his pack, then went on about his business of looking after the cattle ranging in that vicinity.

When spring broke, most of the crew just drifted up White Canyon and out of the country. Silver Tip liked the canyon country and crossed his horses at Dandy Crossing and followed the ledges up Trachyte into the Henry Mountains. Jack Moore was just lining up a crew for the spring ride at the Roost, and Silver Tip hired on—although it is said Jack never paid a cent in wages in all the years he ran the 3B outfit. During the ride, Silver Tip got acquainted with Blue John and Indian Ed Newcomb, and the three traveled the same trails for several years.

Blue John (John Griffith) came into the country from

the opposite direction, riding out of Grand Junction, Colorado, into the Westwater area around Cisco, Utah, where he got a job cooking on the Harris cow outfit. Blue John was never a cowboy, he was a poor rider and preferred a team and wagon to a saddle horse any time. He was a good boatman, however, and fooled around the rivers a little between sojourns with the Roosters. When he was with them it was more often as cook, camp jockey or errand boy, hauling in supplies, or just as a general handyman for the Bunch.

He had worked for the Harrises a year or two before he got mixed up with bad company. He was a medium large man, weighed about 160 pounds (so Ink Harris, one of the boys, said many years later), was about thirty-five years old, light-complexioned, with the peculiar mark of one blue eye and one brown one; hence the name Blue John, bestowed on him by Harris.

Indian Ed Newcomb, the last one of this trio, came in as a horse wrangler with the old Bar X outfit when with Jim Hammel as foreman it shipped several thousand head of cattle into the country from Texas. Newcomb was a tall lad, of about seventeen or eighteen who, Hammel said, was half Cherokee. He looked and acted the part, was dark and somber, with hardly a word to say. Most men at that time could neither read nor write, but Indian Ed wrote a beautiful hand and seemed to be well educated. He also had great artistic ability and was always sketching pictures in the sand with a twig, often drawing the likeness of a man he was talking to as they squatted on a sand bump visiting. This tickled the fellows and gained him their liking where his taciturnity and reserve would have brought him nothing but tolerance, if not downright unfriendliness.

These three, Blue John, Silvertip and Indian Ed, circulated with the Wild Bunch, lending a hand wherever it was needed, whether in bank robbery, horse stealing or whatever was under way. Blue John, as runner for the bunch, brought the women into the Roost the fall of 1896 and drove the wagon out the next spring just before the Castle Gate holdup, taking the women back to Castle Valley from where they returned to their homes.

After Jack Moore was killed by Spicer in Wyoming, Silver
Tip, Blue John and Indian Ed returned to Utah with the
horses they had stolen and took them to Colorado to sell.
Returning to the Roost, they gathered another bunch on the
trail as they traveled along, ending at the Roost with some
choice horseflesh. From the southeastern part of Utah they
had lifted one from Latigo Gordon of Monticello, one from
Mons Peterson at Moab, a mule from the Court House Stage
Station and two horses, one of them a little gray race horse,
from Andrew Tangren of Moab.

This ripped it—too many horses, and the very best in the
country. Tangren started out, with blood in his eye, to trail
the outfit. Sheriff Tyler of Moab was out of town following
a jail breaker, but when he returned, he organized a posse
and left, overtaking Tangren in a day or two near the
town of Green River.

The Moab *Times-Independent* (*Grand Valley Times*,
then) of March 3, 1899, states:

> Sheriff Tyler and posse, Andrew Tangren, J. C. Wilcox,
> H. Day, William Wilson and R. W. Westwood returned
> from a 12 day trip into the San Rafael country after horses
> stolen from Andrew Tangren two weeks ago. They did not
> get the horses they went after, but found two that were
> taken from Joseph Taylor and Thomas Larsen last summer.
>
> The party relate an exciting incident of the trip. In
> trailing up the horses from here, they lost the trail on the
> other side of Green River. Believing they could get assist-
> ance in learning the trails from people farther west, they
> went to Hanksville, but failed to secure any assistance
> there, and went on as far as the Henry Mountains. On
> their return last Monday, at a point about 50 miles south
> of Green River Station they saw fresh trail leading into
> the San Rafael country and followed it up.
>
> When indications were that they were close in on the
> party, they waited until night and located them by their
> campfire, but they were in a side canyon under shelving
> rocks that it was impossible to approach without discovery.
> They kept watch until morning when one of the group, a
> half-breed Indian, came out into the open and was ordered

to throw up his hands, but instead commenced shooting and the sheriff party opened fire on him. He dropped and was last seen crawling behind the rocks. The others came out into the open and one fired a shot into the air and yelled to the sheriff's party to drift, but was answered by a volley. A battle then commenced and lasted for nearly two hours, a hundred or more shots were fired on both sides as far as known without damage. Fire from behind the rocks finally stopped, and the sheriff's party, being nearly out of ammunition, withdrew.

This was a pretty sketchy account of the affair, and reflected a good deal more credit on the posse than anyone else seems inclined to give them. According to reports of people in the country in 1899, and the probabilities suggested by the terrain itself, this is pretty close to what happened.

The outlaws were well aware of the fact that the posse had gone on to Hanksville, but were not too worried about what the lawmen would learn there. While they were on their way from Tidwell Bottoms on the San Rafael River to the Roost they learned from Chris Halverson, a rancher on the San Rafael, that there was law abroad in the land. For the past two or three years, posses had come and gone, being careful not to get too close. Although they were a nuisance, the boys didn't pay much attention to them.

The three outlaws, Blue John, Silver Tip and Indian Ed, with two packhorses and six head of loose horses, pulled into the Roost spring late in the February afternoon, tired and hungry. It was a welcome homecoming; they had even shot an antelope from the bunch they met on the trail among the big sand bumps at the head of Antelope Valley. The hind quarters were tied on the back of Indian Ed's saddle, since he was the lightest in weight of the riders.

They watered their horses at the Roost trough, noting by the tracks of horses and cattle around the spring and on the trails that there were no riders active on the range.

The old camp at Buhr Pass had been abandoned for some time, and passing riders usually camped at the cabin above Roost Spring. This was where they intended to throw off their packs.

The store and stopping place at Hanksville that was run by Charles Gibbons. The little girl in the white dress is the Gibbons' daughter, now Mrs. Mart Robison. She is still living at Hanksville.

—PHOTO COURTESY OF MRS. MART ROBISON, HANKSVILLE, UTAH

Blue John dismounted in the dooryard and opened the door of the cabin. Such a stench of "rat" met him, together with the general closeness of a dirty cabin tightly closed, that he shut the door again, secured the strap latch and returned to his horse.

"Damn rat has built a nest under the bed in the corner," he remarked. "Besides the rest of the place ain't too clean."

"Why don't we go on up and camp at the cave spring?" Silver Tip suggested. "There should be some wood up there, and I don't mind saying I'm hungry and tired."

"Go on," Blue John agreed. "I want to go over here to the blacksmith shop and see if I can locate a pair of shoes that I can tack on Jug's front feet. He's getting a little tender in front." He led his horse toward the ledge, and the other two drove the horses on up the draw.

Locating a couple of horseshoes that he thought he could use, Blue John mounted, trotted up, and overtook the others. They turned north out of the main wash to pick their way

the quarter of a mile or so up the brush-choked side canyon,
where the little sweet spring sweated out of the walls and
floor of the narrow, crack-like cave at the head of the canyon.

The high ledges fell back from the mouth of the cave, but
the canyon was narrow with catclaw and rabbit brush almost choking the trail as it wound up the bottom of the
wash and was forced out from side to side on the banks to
miss rocks and brush. Silver Tip couldn't help thinking as
they threw off the packs that if a posse did follow a bunch
into here what a perfect trap this would be for an ambush.
With the hundred-foot walls completely surrounding the
little open canyon head, a couple of men could look down
into a camp and pick off the campers like beef in a slaughter
pen.

He recalled that just where the east side of the canyon
joined the main Roost Draw, a tongue of sandstone ran
down, and an active man could climb out afoot, but a horseman would have to go around the point and up a side draw
to get away. For a good hundred yards below the spring
cave, the narrow canyon and high walls made a perfect trap.
He wondered why he thought about this. He'd camped here
for years and did not remember ever thinking about it before. Probably the posse that had gone on to Hanksville
had brought it to his mind.

After throwing off the packs and saddles against a big
red sandrock at the mouth of the cave, Indian Ed, who
always took care of the horses while the other two did the
camp work, jumped on his horse bareback and, driving the
other horses, took them around the point to the east and
out on top of the broken draws leading into the main wash.
Here in the sandhills the old sand grass was still high and
thick. The evening was mild, with the promise of an early
spring, and Ed noticed that there were a few green spears
already showing in the bunches of grass, making it more
palatable to the tired, hungry horses.

He hobbled the horses, catching them with a nosebag of
oats, which each horse gobbled greedily while Ed adjusted
the hobbles.

He pulled the bridle off his own mount when he had

finished, and walked back to the ledge above camp, where he left the bridle to pick up the next morning and, following the ledge around to the left of the spring, finally made his way down the steeply sloping rock to the wash below camp.

Silver Tip had the blow-sand and debris cleaned out of the crack in the floor of the cave and a dam built across the front to hold the seepage. Clear, sweet water had collected in the little pools along the crack, each holding a quart or so. Indian Ed got himself a drink then pitched in to help with camp chores. Supper of antelope steaks and dutch-oven biscuits was well on its way, with the coffee just coming to a boil. Picking up a bedroll, he walked to a level place, scraped away the sticks and rocks and spread the bed.

After supper, the three sat for a while around the fire well content, in companionable silence or in low-voiced small talk. Blue John got up to throw a stick of wood on the camp fire.

"Guess I'll have to haul down another load of wood; we're just about out, and I think I was the one who brought this in," he chuckled, remembering what a chore it had been to get the logs snaked up by saddlehorn from the main wash. The trail had been traveled a whole lot more then, and was a good deal wider.

"I don't think we'll ever need it." Silver Tip leaned forward, and held a splinter in the coals to fire up his Bull Durham cigarette. "Looks to me like the old days are about gone."

"I'll bet you're right." Indian Ed brushed the sand between his boot toes smooth again, erasing the picture he had been sketching in the sand with a match stub. "We may never see the day when a posse comes into the Roost, but we sure have seen the time when the boys made a run here." He stood and stretched. "And some of us may even stick around long enough to have to give a posse the slip right here."

They turned in and slept the sound sleep of tired men under the cold winter stars and moon that bathed the canyon in an unearthly light, almost as bright as day.

Just at dawn, when all the earth holds its breath for a second, when all Nature pauses and men who sleep outdoors

Silver Tip Spring, above The Roost, where the battle with the posse was fought by Indian Ed, Silver Tip, and Blue John.

—PHOTO BY PEARL BAKER

snap awake to lie quiescent for a few heartbeats to become attuned to living again, Indian Ed opened his eyes. He rolled out to pull on his pants and boots and go after the horses. Blue John, who always hated to face another day, groaned and settled more firmly under the covers. Silver Tip crawled out, too, and began gathering chips and bark to start the fire.

By the time Ed had reached the point where he could climb out over the rocks, it was getting light. He had climbed slowly and leisurely about halfway out when the peaceful morning was shattered by a burst of rifle fire. Nobody had to draw Indian Ed a map, he fell over, as much from reaction as from the shock of the slug that had ricocheted off the sandrock and struck him just above the knee. He didn't know he was hit until he had rolled back into the draw and crawled into the brush. From there, it was easy enough to get to camp up the sandy wash bottom under the sheltering brush, even dragging a leg.

"How bad you hit?" Silver Tip had grabbed up his rifle and was running down the draw to get a better vantage point from which to return the fire.

"Just flesh, I'll get my gun." And he went on up to camp and picked up his .40-.82. He looked at his leg, and found it bleeding so badly that he decided to put a dressing on it before going back into action.

Blue John had entered the fray with his .45-.70, throwing a few shots toward the posse; then, seeing Silver Tip crawling down toward him from the camp, went to meet him.

"What do you think we better do?" Blue John asked. "We're in a plenty bad spot. Once them fellers get up on the ledge, we're dead pigeons."

"You know it!" agreed Silver Tip. "And I think I better get out on top before they think of it. There I can do a little shooting down on them."

"How?" inquired Blue John practically.

"Right over that point." Tip gestured with the gun.

"Like hell you will. They'll pick you off before you get ten feet from the bottom of the wash."

"They won't if you're keeping them busy enough down here." Tip sat down and pulled off his boots so he could climb faster and more surefootedly over the steep slope. He fastened them with his belt through the pull-loops, hanging them down his back out of the way. By that time, Blue John had crawled up behind a big bush growing on the right hand side of the wash against the ledge. He settled his gun in a notch of the brush stump and began to smoke up the posse and keep them too busy to watch the opposite side of the wash. When he had built up a pretty good barrage, Silver Tip made a run for it, carrying his rifle.

He got part way up the slope before the posse spotted him. With a yell, they laid down a hail of lead all around him. In a zigzagging burst of speed, he made the lip of the ledge, and dropped back of the rim to heave in a couple of good, deep breaths. Then he stuck his head around a blackbrush growing in a crack in the edge of the ledge and looked the situation over.

There were six or seven men grouped down in the main Roost Draw, behind a couple of big catclaw bushes about three hundred yards away. The horses were being held farther down by a couple of men, and he could see those two fellows were having their troubles with the horses milling and trying to break loose.

Silver Tip was an old hand at this game. In all his outlaw days he had never killed a man, and he didn't intend to start now unless he was forced to. But the situation demanded drastic measures. He drew a careful bead just over the posse—but close—and cut loose. At about the third shot placed too near, the posse broke and fled. Mounting their spooky horses and whipping over and under, the posse raced down the draw toward the Roost Spring.

Blue John quit bombarding the vacated position and went back to camp, where Silver Tip had walked to the edge of the ledge just above, and was watching Indian Ed stir up the breakfast fire.

"If I'd had Red Bird saddled, I'd have made them travel a damn sight faster," Silver Tip offered from his vantage point above the camp.

"You might be right." Blue John pushed his hat back and leaned back to look up. "But from what I saw, not very much faster."

"Think they'll come back?"

"Not a chance. They'll make plenty tracks right back to Mom and stick their feet back into the oven until time to start plowing, make no mistake about that. Besides, they've got a dandy story to tell now."

"I'll get the horses while I'm up here," Silver Tip offered, and since Ed's leg was beginning to hurt, he agreed.

At breakfast, the three men soberly discussed what the future held.

"As far as I can see," Silver Tip said, "this is it. I'm getting out while I can still travel."

"Me, too," agreed Blue John, "and I think we better split up right here."

"Good idea," Silver Tip agreed. "But we only got two pack outfits. We can split the camp, but two of us are going to have to stick together for a while, anyway."

"Count me out." Indian Ed spoke up. "I'm not going to ride very far or fast for several days. I'll go on over to Hanksville, and lay around there somewhere until my leg gets all right. You two take the packs."

There was a pause, and the other two fellows looked at him. Noticing this, he said, "You take the horses, too. I'm plumb through with this kind of life. And if I can get out of this scrape, this finishes my outlaw days."

Silver Tip set down his coffee cup and looked at Ed with relief. "So that's what's eating you," he remarked. "I knew something was bitin' you, but I couldn't figure out what it was. I figured it was because you were sore at one of us for something, and I'm glad it's not that."

"That's not it." Ed stood up and closed his knife, after wiping the antelope steak grease off the blade. "But I hate this running business. I should have left before. Now I may not have a chance." His dark streak of Indian pessimism held him.

"Aw, you'll be all right." Blue John started to pick up the meager camp. "How shall we divide this outfit?"

There was some argument, no one wanting to take more than his share, and Indian Ed holding out stubbornly for none of it at all. But they finally got the camp split, and the two packhorses loaded.

Blue John had no further interest in the horses, he was going to take his packhorse and with one extra saddle horse, drop down the North Trail, follow along Under the Ledge and cross the Colorado River at Spanish Bottoms. There he would go out toward Colorado.

"Be damned if I'm going to leave all these horses we

have had so much trouble stealing this winter," Silver Tip
declared. He and Indian Ed started toward Hanksville, Silver Tip intending to cross the Colorado at Lee's Ferry and
go into Arizona, and possibly on to Old Mexico.

That fall Blue John, who was an expert boatman, came
to Hite where, being an expert on the river, he departed for
Lee's Ferry by boat. He was never heard from again, which
doesn't mean he came to grief on the river. It probably
means he left the river above Lee's Ferry and went south,
to be lost on some lonely ranch in Arizona or among the
isolated villages of Mexico.

Silver Tip and Indian Ed had not traveled toward Hanksville very far when they cut the tracks of a herd of sheep.
That was good enough for Ed. Before Silver Tip was aware
he had changed his mind, he stopped off his horse, tied up
the reins and while rolling a smoke said:

"This is where I leave you. I can hide out until my leg
heals. I'll be pretty stiff by tomorrow or next day, but I
can manage to overtake these sheep. And I don't want that
stolen horse and saddle to fool with. I'll take my gun." And
he went limping along the sheep tracks.

He heard Silver Tip put the horses on the trail again,
and stopped once to look back over his shoulder as they
dipped over a ridge and dropped out of sight. His leg was
just loosening up so he could travel when he came in sight
of the sheep camp.

Charl Hanks (Neil's younger brother) and two fellows,
Hy Bjorensen and Jim Watt, were herding the sheep, which
belonged to L. George and Ed Tuttle. The sheepherders
extended the common hospitality of the range and Indian
Ed stayed with them for about two weeks, although he was
so ringy and nervous all the time he finally had them pretty
much on edge.

Fifty years later Charl remembered that when the camp
set on a hill where Ed could look around, he was more or
less at ease, particularly if the sheep were quiet. But if the
sheep were restless, as they sometimes were at that time
of year, Ed would be up and down all night, listening to
the bells and imagining that all kinds of posses were sneaking up on him, scaring the sheep.

One night the camp was pitched down in a deep valley,

almost a hole, and the sheep bedded around it. Indian Ed
had protested. He couldn't see around during the late evening and felt hemmed in. About midnight the sheep "ran,"
probably from some predator, a coyote or bobcat, and the
men had to get up and herd them back. Ed didn't close his
eyes the rest of the night and held his gun in his hands
until daylight.

His leg healed but he kept rubbing it. One morning as
they were getting out of bed, Charl remarked, "Ed, that
looks festered. I'll bet there's a piece of cloth or something
in it."

"That we can soon see," answered Ed and, opening his
knife, he slashed open the scar and removed a flattened
.38-.55 slug.

A few days later, his leg almost healed, he thanked the
boys one morning and, as they started up the draw, he
went down on foot. Around the bend of the draw and up a
side gully he picked up his hobbled horse, which he hadn't
wanted the boys to see, saddled up and rode away south
and east toward the Roost.

They saw him riding away, however, and returned to read
the story in the tracks, but they never knew how he had
sent word out to have the horse brought to him, nor who
had brought it. It was thought that he returned to Okla-
homa, but he was never heard from again.

Not all of the horse thieves belonged to the Wild Bunch.
The *Grand Valley Times* of March 24, 1899, states:

> Sheriff Tyler with H. Day, Andrew Tangren, Wm. Little-
> ly and Harvey Hancock left the first of the week to look
> for stolen horses in the San Rafael country. It was re-
> ported Wednesday that Tyler had located the parties with
> which they had the fight some weeks ago, and had sent
> word to the sheriff of Carbon County for aid. It was
> learned that the Indian was seriously hurt in the first fight.

April 1, 1899:

> Sheriff Tyler and posse returned Wednesday evening
> from a trip into the San Rafael country after stolen horses
> and horse thieves. They brought in 8 horses and one mule.

The mule had been stolen from Mr. Young at the Court
House Rock State Station, one horse from Mons Peterson
and one from W. E. Gordon at Monticello. The others an
owner is wanted for.

A description of the horses followed. An owner was found
for the horses much sooner than the posse anticipated—
Mrs. Jack Moore.

September 29, 1899:

When Sheriff Tyler and posse went into the San Rafael
country last spring, they brought back a number of horses
that had been stolen from this vicinity, among them two
horses that had been rode (sic) by 'Silver Tip' and party
when in Moab. Mrs. Moore, wife of Jack Moore, for whose
arrest the Governor has offered a reward of $500, has
brought suit against Sheriff Tyler for $2100 for having
taken these horses. Such is what an officer has to contend
against that is doing his duty, and while no respectable
court is likely to find a judgment against the sheriff for
bringing in stolen property of citizens, such suits cause
him unnecessary expense and trouble. It is just such actions that discourage officers from doing their duty, and it
seems strange that attorneys in good standing can be
found to father such suits.

Later editions of the paper report that Tyler went over
to Wayne County to stand trial, but no mention is made of
the disposition of the case. Likely he took the horses back
to their owner and the matter was dropped.

Law enforcement enjoyed quite a surge of life that spring,
with Joe Bush, Ott Thompson and Jack Cottrell taking the
trail of Silver Tip, who was working his way peaceably out
of the country. Apparently he had lost a part of his herd
containing the mule and the Mons Peterson horse, which
the posse found and returned to Moab. The three possemen
followed Silver Tip until he stopped for the night in an
abandoned cabin about forty miles north of Lee's Ferry.

They knew well enough that an outlaw slept with his

gun close at hand, but was pretty apt to be careless before he got his eyes well opened for the day. They bedded down outside the cabin, and waited for morning. Just at daylight they heard a stirring in the cabin and presently Silver Tip emerged into the crisp spring morning. Just as he stepped through the door and turned to his right, he found himself face to face with Jack Cottrell. He whirled to make a dive back through the door, but found Ott Thompson directly in front of him.

"Don't move or I'll shoot!" yelled Cottrell, which didn't stop Silver Tip. Jack shot but missed—both Silver Tip and Thompson, luckily. There wasn't much else to do, so Silver Tip surrendered.

The posse felt they had really caught a bad one, one of the Robbers Roosters who had laughed at the law for a long time. They loaded him into a wagon at Kanab and took him over the mountain to Beaver, where the ankle chains were left locked on him while he made his way up the court-house steps before the awed populace. His preliminary hearing was held at Beaver, but he was taken into Provo for safe keeping. However, when he was tried in 1900, it was at Loa, county seat of Wayne County. He was sentenced to a term in the State Penitentiary. He had said very little about himself, and since there was no way to connect him with any outlawry, he was charged with resisting arrest.

The *Grand Valley Times,* June 9, 1899, states:

> Howells, alias Hawkins, alias 'Silver Tip,' one of the party that made the fight on Sheriff Tyler and posse in the San Rafael country last March has been captured by Joe Bush and posse about 40 miles north of Lee's Ferry near the Colorado River. He will be taken to Loa, Wayne County, for trial on the charge of attempted murder. Sheriff Tyler and one or more of the party that was with him in the fight will go to Loa to appear against him. 'Silver Tip' had with him a .30-.30 Winchester believed to have formerly belonged to Moab parties. He had 10 head of horses with him when captured. It was not learned whether horses stolen from Moab parties were among them.

September 29, 1900.

> Howells, alias 'Silver Tip' was convicted at Loa on last
> Tuesday of a charge of assault with intent to commit mur-
> der and sentenced to a term of ten years in the state prison.
> The crime for which he was convicted was last March in
> the San Rafael country when he and three others fought
> Sheriff Tyler and posse from Grand County who were
> chasing horse thieves who had been operating in this
> county. The other parties have not yet been caught.

The *Sun-Advocate* at Price reported on January 19, 1901:

> Silver Tip Howells, or Hawkins, Wayne County's noted
> criminal, released from the pen recently on a writ of Ha-
> beas Corpus proved too foxy for Sheriff Hancock at Torrey
> last week and is now at large. While awaiting a preliminary
> hearing, the sheriff allowed Howells to occupy a room by
> himself overnight, and found next morning his bird had
> flown. Howells had served less than two years of a ten-
> year sentence. He has not been recaptured.

And he never was. He had played a minor role in the
saga of the Wild Bunch, he wasn't much wanted by the law,
and it cost more to prosecute him than it was really worth.
He drifted over into Brown's Park and finally up into Wyoming, where he spent the rest of his life—very quietly it
seems. He was never bothered again by the law officers.

While these three, Blue John, Indian Ed and Silver Tip
kept things stirred up pretty well for a few years, twenty
years earlier a different triumvirate had been riding high
and handsome. However, the crime life of the McCarty family got nipped in the bud rather early—and with great
finality.

TOM, BILLY
AND
FRED McCARTY

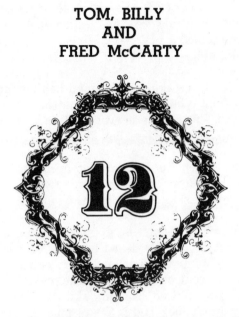

Gene Grimes (no relation to the Grimes of Chapter 10, but a member of a respectable family of western Colorado whose descendants live in that area to this day) had bought a horse from Tom McCarty early in the summer of 1893, but what with putting the cattle on the La Sals, branding the calves, and getting the haying done in Paradox Valley, he hadn't found time to round the horse out of the Sinbad country down on the Dolores River in western Colorado. Work slacked off a little in September, and on the 8th, a blustery, windy day, Gene rode down to the abandoned ranch on the bank of Dolores, where he intended to spend the night, then find the horse and return the following day.

When he dismounted near the front corner of the little one-room log cabin in the cedars and stepped over to the door, he happened to glance down at the trail from the door to the cellar built in a cutbank a few feet away. He noticed there were fresh boot tracks in the trail. The cabin was used to some extent by cowboys and other riders, and one of the local cow outfits kept staple supplies there for the

149

convenience of their hands, who used it for a line camp. Gene decided to go over to the cellar and find out who his camping partner would be. The cellar door was almost closed, which seemed a little odd, but he pushed it in, stood in the opening and—looked right down the barrel of a .30-.30 Winchester!

He immediately recognized the man behind the gun and said, "Hello, Tom. What the hell's the matter with you?"

"Hello, Gene. I'm a little nervous." Tom McCarty let the gun move aside a few inches, but didn't lower it. "Come on in."

Gene pushed back his hat, and stepped into the cellar, stooping under the low roof. Tom moved forward, and, much to Gene's surprise slapped him on the side for a shoulder holster.

"Never carry one, Tom," he grinned. "Always carry my shootin' irons right outside. But I bet I haven't carried anything but a saddle gun for venison for five years."

The two men went outside, and Gene looked at the older man closely. Tom looked bad, his skin was putty-colored, and his eyes didn't look right. There must be some reason for it, Gene figured, so he'd just let things rock along for a time and see what was up. He knew that Tom was pretty fast on the trigger, and that he often rode the dim trails, but news hadn't traveled as fast as McCarty had that day, and Gene hadn't yet heard about the Delta Bank robbery. He didn't know that Tom was pretty shaken by the failure, that he had heard one shot and that his brother and nephew, Billy and Fred McCarty, had not followed him. For the first time in a long career of robbery, things had gone entirely against him, and he couldn't recover his balance.

The two entered the cabin and cooked a simple supper, using the staples there and what Gene had brought in his saddle bags. Tom stayed close to his gun and watched out of the door and the one window all the time.

After they had eaten, Tom pushed back his chair, rolled and lit a cigarette and said, "Guess you haven't heard what happened yesterday."

Gene admitted that he was a little short on news, and would sure like to know what was going on. Tom told him about the story of the bank robbery at Delta.

"You go back to Paradox and tell Letty, Billy's wife, any-thing you're a mind to, but I don't know what happened. They either both got arrested—or killed. I heard that one shot, and two more when I had got pretty well out of town, and I know as well as I'm sitting here that they didn't make it. I just got a feeling that they were both killed.

"She oughta go over to Delta, or send someone, to see they get a decent burial. I know I can never go back. In fact, as soon as it gets dark, I'm leaving the country, and I don't rightly know where I'll go."

"Better wait until I run in that bunch of horses tomor-row. I'd imagine your horse was about used up today."

Tom agreed, and Gene suggested they roll in. Tom showed his nervousness again, and finally Gene agreed to take the few blankets out in the cedars and bed down in case the law officers rode up in the night. Gene undressed as he had done for several years in camp, his hat first, his boots to weight it down and his socks spread to dry over them. He slid out of his pants and folded them to put under the thin pillow.

Tom's toilet was simpler. He weighted his hat down with a rock and slid into bed, his rifle under his hand at the side of the bed.

Gene hardly knew what to think. He could see that Tom had every right to be shaky and scared, but he couldn't imagine a man's not settling down for a night's sleep, par-ticularly since the next day promised some strain.

The wind had gone down with the sun, and the night was cool and clear with a promise of early frost. The stars seemed to swing low as if to hear the stories that Tom told all night long. He seemed filled with the need to make it clear to his companion where he had gone wrong and why.

Gene dozed from time to time, but wakened when Tom talked.

Tom started the tale with when he was a boy in central Utah, near Salina, growing up as most Mormon boys did in a poor family.

"We were kinda wild, even as kids, and didn't spend much time on the ranch. My grandmother sort of raised us, and when I was about eighteen, I married Tiny Christiansen, Matt Warner's sister. You know Matt, don't you?"

Gene acknowledged with a drowsy grunt that he did.

"A few years ago the Maxwell and Ray families pulled in there with their wagons, coming back from California. They had come originally from Tennessee, crossed the plains, and camped in Denver when it was just a saloon on Cherry Creek, I've heard them say. They went on to California, but came back to Utah. I never could see why. They wanted to have a cow outfit, and they hadn't found what they needed in California.

"About that time the Mormon Church was trying to get people to settle in this part of the country to try to tame the Indians. They were pretty bad, the Indians. The Navajos raided southern Utah regularly. The Church authorities decided that if a few white families came out here, it would civilize the Indians faster.

"That wasn't the reason the Rays and Maxwells came over here, although it did have a bearing. We heard there was good cow feed in this part of the country, good winter range, and the La Sals for summer grazing. With other families in the country it looked like a good deal, and we came on over. I didn't have much to bring, but Billy had married one of the Maxwell girls, and I just come along with them.

"Your family got here a couple of years ago, didn't they?" he asked Gene.

"Yeah, from Colorado."

"We had just got Coyote Creek and La Sal Creek settled good when the Pittsburgh Cattle Company come in and bought us out. Maxwells went to Oregon for a while, then back here to Paradox. Billy and I took our families and went along, but we drifted back last spring.

"We pulled some jobs around Oregon, and had to hunt new range. Fred had got shot in a holdup there, so we sent him back on the stage. Took us about a month to bring the horses down."

The two men smoked for a while in silence, then Gene asked how Tom had got started in outlawry.

"The first holdup I pulled was so easy it just about ruined

my life," Tom replied. "It was in Denver, and one of the banks refused to cash a check for me. The check wasn't any good, but they didn't know that—so I decided to hold them up.

"I got a minister's outfit together and rented a room upstairs in the building next to the bank. Then I went into the bank with a pint flask of water, showed it to the teller in one of the cages and told him it was nitroglycerine and, if he didn't give me all the money in his cage, I would throw it on the floor and blow us all to Kingdom Come—and warned him to real quiet about it.

"He came through handsomely, put the money into a bag I handed him, and I turned and walked out of the bank with no one the wiser. I dodged into this room next door, got into the minister's suit and was back on the street again before the alarm had been broadcast too much. I helped hunt the bandit, made it a point to talk face to face with the teller and he didn't recognize me.

"I traveled all over the West then, part of the time with other fellows and some of the time alone. I spent a winter in Star Valley with Matt Warner. We got along fine in those days.

"I haven't seen him since we met in Idaho along a canyon trail. Sure was glad to see him, but Matt's bragging always did make me tired. He'd just held up a payroll, and while we sat there on our horses, he told me two or three times how easy it was to take money away from people. Finally I decided to teach him a lesson, so I just pulled out my gun and said, 'You sure are right, Matt. It's plenty easy to take money from people. You hand over that bunch you got there in your hand, and go take some more away from somebody.' Before he could do anything about it, I reached out, got the money, turned and rode off. I looked back just before I rounded the bend of the trail and he was just sitting there with his mouth open. Probably don't like me anymore.

"We never could have rode the owlhoot trail if it hadn't been for the ranchers and stockmen liking us and helping us out. It was partly to their advantage to do that; ranches were a long way apart, and if a man didn't play along, he could have been killed and his ranch burned. At that time it would have been laid onto Indians.

"But that wasn't the only reason they liked to have us ride in. We usually had quite a bit of news to tell, and ranching was sure a lonesome life. Then we had time to stay and help out for a few days, usually.

"I remember Kid Curry stopped on the ford of the Grand River at Moab. He was just going to camp out there with no outfit, but the Taylors invited him right into the house, and told him to take care of his horse, too.

"The Kid was a good worker, and you know how a ranch is. He stayed around about a week and really made a hand. They didn't know him, and I promised him not to tell who he was—wouldn't look right for one of us boys to be wrastlin' a shovel."

Tom was silent for a time. Then he told a story that Gene, when he heard it again and again about other outlaws in later years, came to wonder if he had heard the original event, or whether Tom was trying to excuse his desertion of the boys at Delta.

"Then we helped out in other ways, too. One time I was coming up from New Mexico and stopped at a ranch I hadn't been to for three or four years. In that time the man had died, and the woman was trying to get along by herself and raise the three kids. She had the best location in that part of the state, good grass and a nice stream of water that run right through most of her range, and finally through her homestead. It was a good outfit but rundown a lot when I pulled in.

"She was glad to see me, but there didn't seem to be much to eat in the place and it looked poor. I couldn't figure it out until she told me her husband had been sick a long time and it had cost them a lot of money. The banker had always wanted the ranch to build a summer home on, so had loaned them the money and was coming out the next day to foreclose the mortgage.

"I had plenty of money on me, usually do have, so I gave her the cash to pay off the mortgage. She didn't want to take it, but I told her it would be all right, wouldn't cost me anything.

"The next day I hid in the cedars and watched the banker ride in to collect his money. I couldn't hear what was said, but I could see he sure didn't like the deal a bit, when he had to give her back the mortgage. Don't rightly know why he had it along, really. Just to gloat over her, I guess.

"I made it a point to meet him down the trail a piece, and we had a little visit that cost him the profit on the deal. I didn't go back to the ranch, but she must have heard what happened, and I've often wondered what she thought about it.

"I traveled all over the West then. *What's that?*"

He raised up quickly in bed, listened a moment and got quietly to his feet. Gene raised up on his elbow and listened.

"It's just cows coming in to water," Gene said. "Remember, the trail up on the bench goes right up this draw."

"Keep still, it might be horses—with riders on them. It could be a posse. Cows don't travel in such big bunches."

Gene listened again, heard the crunch of gravel on the trail, the knock of dew claws. Presently the warm fragrance of cattle drifted up the little slope through the cedars to him.

"Oh, come on back to bed, Tom. You can even smell the cattle, down here next to the ground."

Tom settled down uneasily again. He sat and listened a few more minutes. A cow coughed and another lowed for her calf. A calf frolicked beside the trail, giving a short sharp brr! of mock fear as it kicked at a bush.

Gene dropped off to sleep for a while, how long he didn't know. But he was wakened abruptly when Tom raised up in bed, gun in hand, and sent a bullet screaming through the trees.

"What is it?" Gene spoke just above a whisper in the silence that followed the shot.

"Something or someone sneaking around over there," Tom whispered back. They watched the opening between the cedars for a few minutes, but there was no further activity they could see.

"Just a coyote, I guess," Tom said. The usual chorus of howls and night noises began once more, tentatively at first, then swelling in full volume. "Long as they yell, guess there won't be any riders around," Tom opined hopefully, and the two men settled back once more.

"If there was," Gene informed him caustically, "they would sure know where to find you. Here we are out in the brush on this rocky ground, when we could be in the cabin and comfortable. All so that you can hide out. And what do you do? Blast everything that moves. Now, when we get these cigarettes smoked, I want some sleep."

"Okay—guess we could both use some shut-eye," Tom agreed. He smoked quietly for a few drags. "But you know, Gene, the deeper you get into this outlaw business, the less chance you got to pull out and make something of yourself. I bet I've met every man who ever held up a bank or payroll in the whole West. Not all of 'em live to go straight, but some do. I guess the smart ones—or the lucky ones." He chuckled.

"Now you take Matt Warner. He never was too much of an outlaw, and yet he spent more time in jail for his wrong-doing than all the rest of us put together. But Matt's likely the only one of us who will go straight." But Gene was already asleep, so Tom settled down and slept fitfully.

The two rolled out just before daylight and, while Tom cooked breakfast, Gene went after the horses. He was lucky; the animals he had come to find were with the hobbled saddle horses, and he drove them into the little corral by the cabin. After eating and cleaning up the cabin, the two men saddled up and mounted.

"Well, boy, I don't know where I'm going," Tom said by way of farewell. "But I'm too well known to stay in this country any more. I'll hear somewhere down the line what happened yesterday or the day before, rather, in Delta. If Billy and Fred were killed, people might just forget me, but I doubt it. I'll probably never live a normal life again. Tell Letty what you think she should know."

Gene rode back to Paradox, where he took the message to Letty that her husband and son were probably killed at Delta. It was decided to let her brother, Philander Maxwell, go there and see what was to be done. He was gone about a week, and returned, saying he had seen the two bodies buried in the Delta cemetery. He told her about the holdup.

Tom wasn't the only one hunted from then on. Letty used to go to Oregon to visit her people every year or two, and she often told how she was always followed. But she didn't know where Tom was, never saw him again. She finally moved to Nevada where another son, Eck, had gone to get away from the notoriety, and lived there the rest of her life.

Tom spoke truer than he knew when he said he never would be able to live a normal life again. The Pinkerton detectives were on the job by then, and he never dared show himself.

Oldtimers tell that he spent some time with his son Len McCarty in Green River, Utah, where Len owned a saloon. Some of them claimed to have caught glimpses of him. Bud Milton told about going with Len to see a race horse in a stable back of his home, and an old man was sitting on the screened back porch. When they came in sight he went back into the house, and Len didn't mention anything about him to Bud.

The legend persists that Tom McCarty lived in the Book Cliffs, above Green River, and when he wanted supplies he kindled a fire out on a point which the boys in Green River, Len and Lew, could see, and they would take him food and necessaries. Some claim that he died in the camp up there somewhere.

But the most logical conclusion is that he never was too far from Len and died in California at Len's home. Howard Grimes, a brother of Gene's (according to the story told to me many years later by Mrs. Bertha Ray, their sister), said that one time when he was visiting Len in California, there was an old man living there who seemed to do just as he pleased about the place. Howard was not introduced, and when he asked Len who it was, was told it was just an old fellow who made his home on the ranch. The "old fellow" seemed to know an awful lot about people in Colorado, Howard noticed, and probably could have told an interesting tale about the Telluride and Delta bank robberies, "if he'd been a mind to."

THE TELLURIDE
BANK ROBBERY

Telluride, Colorado, lies in a little cup on the western slope of the Rockies, with its mines high above it on the mountainsides. When I was there the last of June, there were still vast snowbanks on the towering mountains that leaned above it, and waterfalls cascaded down every gulch and cliff.

It was here that the practical application of electricity and transmission of high voltage were first perfected, but that is another story—and a fascinating one.

The townsite was first settled by miners in 1878, and it was then called Columbia. That summer San Miguel County was set apart by the state legislature, and the next year the Board of Trustees changed the "name of said town of Columbia to the Town of Telluride." Some say the name, which originated, of course, from the type of ore mined there, is short for "t'hell you ride" which gives some idea of the character of that booming town in the early days.

Names of the rich old surrounding mines are well

known: Smuggler, Liberty Bell, Black Bear, Alta, Double Eagle (from which not a pound of ore was ever shipped), and while they were running wide open, so was Telluride—with a fabulous payroll, and men not afraid to spend it.

Of course, the camp, being so far from any large town and having so much money circulating, had a bank—the San Miguel Valley Bank. The building is no longer there, but it stood just below where the drugstore is today, back off the street. The newly organized county had some sort of agreement with the bank to furnish office space for the county offices, in the lobby of the bank. Charles Painter was the county clerk, and he and one bank teller by the name of Hyde were the only ones in the bank when it was robbed late in the morning of June 24, 1889. All of the officials had gone to lunch, except Mr. Hyde, who was in his place in the cage, with Mr. Painter at work at his desk.

Suddenly two men, Matt Warner and Butch Cassidy, with handkerchiefs over their faces, entered the bank and demanded the money. The clerk didn't feel called upon to argue with men as well armed and businesslike as these two. He meekly gathered up all the money in the cage— $21,000—and handed it to them. They turned, ran for their horses, being held in the street by Tom McCarty, mounted and rode out of town at a run.

While horses were common in town, three men racing down the valley created a little interest, particularly after one of them snapped a shot at a youngster, Ed Weller, standing on the sidewalk. This was pure bravado and the only shot fired during the holdup, but it sure put speed in young Weller's heels.

The posse gathered immediately under Sheriff Baty, and set off after the robbers as they pounded down the river and turned off to climb Keystone Hill. The story is told that one of the posse, who had a particularly fine saddle horse, grew so enthusiastic that he whipped out in the lead of the others by a couple of hundred yards. Suddenly he looked up and saw he was much too close to the outlaws and a whole lot too far ahead of the supporting posse. With what he considered quick wit and good judgment, he succumbed to a call of nature—but he never heard the last of it. Every time the bank robbers were mentioned for years, some wit would tell how near he came to capturing the whole band of outlaws, and why he didn't.

The posse streamed past him, and on to the foot of Keystone Hill, at the top of which Kid Brown (Bert Madden) was holding the horses for the first change the outlaws considered they would need. He rolled rocks down on the posse, while the outlaws slapped their saddles on fresh horses and made tracks.

Another story is that Madden had caught a wild horse while he was waiting, and when he saw how closely the posse followed, he tied a good-sized tree to the horse's tail and started him down the trail. The horses of the posse stampeded into the brush, and by the time they could get organized again, it was too late to give chase on winded horses to desperate men on fresh mounts. That the race was close is borne out by the fact that a few months later cowboys found four horse carcasses still tied to a tree. They had been left for a relay, but the outlaws, crowded into a different getaway, had been unable to pick them up.

A big black horse was left at the top of Keystone Hill because he was too winded even to be driven in the bunch of loose horses that Bill Madden herded away. This horse was branded CT on the thigh and was always called Keystone by Jim Clarke, who brought him home and used him for a couple of years. One morning Jim went out to the corral and Keystone had disappeared in the night.

Bill Madden held the main bunch of horses and drove them to a ranch nearby. The posse caught him and he spent some time in jail, but Bert was never apprehended.

The outlaws raced toward Ophir, turning off just a little north of Trout Lake. There they spent a couple of weeks secure in the Lizard Head country, near Lone Cone, on Fisher Mesa. Then they went down through Beaver Park.

A few days later, on the fifth of July to be exact, they held up a train at Stoney Creek. An old cowpuncher, Roy Dickerson ("Little Dick"), who was raised in Dolores, Colorado, and worked for us at the Roost for years, off and on, told this story:

I went down to Dolores for the 4th of July. I was just a kid then, dayherding cattle. The next morning the boss pulled me off the dayherd, where I was watching some old mosshorn steers McGraw was gathering out of the oak brush, and sent me down to help brand some calves at the siding on Stoney Creek.

While we were working in the corral that also served as loading pens on the railroad, a fellow rode up and climbed over on the fence. Pretty soon he asked what time the train came along. We told him at 1:00 o'clock.

A few minutes later we heard the whistle of the train. The fellow got down off the fence, and we heard him talking to someone. Pretty soon along came two more and this fellow, on some damn good horses. They tied their mounts up over across the track, in some trees. When the train came along, they took a shot at the engineer to stop the train. They were down behind the section house, and we couldn't see very good. We weren't trying to see too much; thought it might not be healthy. But we did notice a couple of fishermen come up the creek in their wading boots and go snooping over to see what was going on. The train robbers just jumped them around in line with the passengers, and robbed them, too.

We couldn't stand it any longer, and sneaked over where we could hear better. But we didn't stay long, and kept down out of sight, you bet. I heard one big kid say, "I sure hope they don't hurt Maw," and he looked toward the train. I guess she hadn't got off with the passengers lined up beside the cars. But I don't think they even missed Maw; they were pretty busy.

When it was about over, we got back to branding calves, and when the outlaws rode past, they all said, "Hello, boys," and went right on about their business. The one that had been on the fence was clean shaven, but there was one of them with a red beard. We'd noticed that the one on the fence hadn't had much of a hat, either, just an old sloppy one with the brim tucked up under on each side so it wouldn't lop down and cut off his seeing. When they went past, he had on a brand new Stetson.

One of our neighbors was on the train, and he got

robbed, too. He didn't get back on the train, but come swearing over to the corral, and we loaned him a horse to ride home on. He told us that he had had his new hat stolen the night before at the dance, so he had bought a new one that morning to wear back to the ranch. He got on the train and the outlaw fancied this new Stetson so took it, too. J. W. didn't have a gun, but he opined that the next sonofabitch that took a hat off him was going to be a helluva fast shot, and would be robbing a corpse.

There were four of the fellows that had robbed the bank at Telluride. They camped in the mouth of West Fork, but only three of them robbed the train. One fellow had taken their extra horses about forty miles around the day before, and they cut through, robbed the train and met him on the Dolores River. Me and another kid followed the tracks out.

They left three horses in the country when they pulled out, horses that had carried them part of the trail from Telluride and were pretty badly give out. There was a sorrel T Lazy E 帀 ; a gray CD Bar **CD** and a black Boxed Heart ♥ horse. The black was a ringtail.* Then there was a black horse with CT or TC on his thigh that we always called Keystone. He was left at the top of Keystone Hill.

I've heard people say that those fellows rode the same horses from Telluride to the head of Mancos, over Chicken Creek Divide, down on to the Dolores into Moab. That's wrong. They went down the trail and out to Beaver Park.

Things were getting a shade warm, so the boys decided to leave the country. They pulled into the river crossing of the Colorado at Moab, just before daylight. The Taylors owned the ferry. As Don Taylor told it many years later:

> One night my father, Lester Taylor, and his son Jick, and some of the rest of the family were sleeping out on the hills above the river where the ferry was moored. They

---

* A horse that switches his tail and actually whips it around and around—a most annoying habit—is called a "ringtail" by cowboys.

often slept up there where the mosquitoes were not so bad and where it was cooler. Jick woke up as some men rode up and asked to be taken across the river. The boys said they would have to wait until morning, it was too dangerous to cross in the dark with the river high with spring run-off.

Matt Warner answered, "Our business lies rolling. We've got to get across the river."

My father was awake by that time, and recognized the voice, and said, "Come on, we will put them across."

Many years later, during Prohibition, several men from Moab were attending court in Emery County. It was late in the fall, the roads were bad, and it was storming and cold when they pulled into Price. They had been on the road seven hours since leaving Moab, and they were tired, cold, and hungry—and felt they could sure use a drink of whiskey.

The matter was mentioned, and one of the Taylors said, "Matt Warner lives in town, works some place here, and if we can find him, I think we can get a drink."

Someone told them where Matt worked in a pool hall. They asked him if he could get them anything to drink, and he, not recognizing the Taylors, started naming off the different kinds of soda pop he had. Taylor said, looking Matt right in the eye, "Matt, just like you were one morning before daylight on the Grand River, *our business lies rolling!*"

Warner immediately recognized him, and called someone to take his place, saying that he was on the wrong side of that bar. He took the boys in hand, and they threw a beautiful party, recalling the good old days when Matt and Butch rode fast horses long distances.

He told them that the group had split up shortly after crossing the Grand (Colorado) that time long ago. He and Tom rode into Brown's Park, and Butch wandered up into Wyoming.

The Taylors knew part of the story that followed, how, after moving around the country for a few years, the Mc-Cartys had come back into the western Colorado area some four years later, in 1893, robbing the bank at Delta.

THE DELTA
BANK ROBBERY

In a few cases the story of getting material is almost as
interesting as the material I found. In Delta, Colorado,
in 1957, after I had spent a day or two interviewing people and checking the records, someone sent me to see Ben
Laycock, who lived in a little cabin behind a store across
the street from the depot.

I knocked on his door early in the morning. It was such
a beautiful morning that we decided to sit on a bench outside his door and visit. There, in the coolness of a typical
Colorado summer forenoon, he told me the story of the
Delta bank robbery as he remembered it. Never having
heard a robbery account from the viewpoint of a twelve-
year-old boy, I sat spellbound as he carried us back sixty-
four years to the afternoon of September 7, 1893:

> My father ran the photography shop, and when I was
> about twelve, he took my brother Henry into partnership,
> calling the shop F. M. Laycock and Son. I wasn't included
> in the partnership, but at that time we used a process of
> chloride of gold to tone the pictures, called Aristo Prints,
> and they had to be washed and washed for hours. I wasn't

supposed to have anything to do, so you can guess who washed prints day after day.

On the afternoon of the robbery I was on the east stoop of the photo shop, where it was cool, bathing prints and witnessed all the actions in my range of vision, and learned the rest of the facts later.

About the first of September, 1893, three strangers came into town, spending most of their time in the Steve Bailey Saloon, the "Palace Sampling Rooms" just across the street from the Farmers and Merchants Bank of Delta. They were checking on the possibilities of robbing the bank, but no one knew it then. They played cards and drank with the other men of the saloon until the afternoon of the seventh.

After a big mid-day meal at "Bricktop's Cafe," 251 Main Street, they seemed a bit more nervous than usual, and about half past three, Tom McCarty said to Billy and Fred, "It's about time to get started."

The other two agreed, and Tom went out the back door to get the horses, tied in the alley behind the saloon. Mounting his own and leading the other two he turned down the alley south, going to Fourth Street, across Main to the alley east of Main, then north to the rear of the bank, where he got off and held the three horses.

A lean-to had been built on the back of the bank building, just a small room, and W. R. Robertson used it for a law office. The back door was so low that the screen door swung in instead of out on it. Back of the lean-to was a coal bin with two posts stuck up to hold up a roof that was no longer there. Tom waited here by this coal bin for the other two to come out of the bank.

Billy McCarty and his son Fred came out of the saloon, jaywalked across Main Street to the bank on the east side of the street at 316 Main. Their shadows were cast through the windows to the bank floor in the part in front of the partition, but none of the bank people even noticed them especially.

The McCartys opened the door and walked straight to the seven-foot partition, and started to climb over. They told the bank employees to be quiet, and not to holler, if they valued their lives, and to hand over all the funds. At this point, Andrew Blachly let out a yell, and Fred leveled his sixgun on Blachly and killed him, the bullet going through him and into the floor.

The McCartys got down off the railing on the inside and proceeded to rake in the greenbacks and stuff them into their shirt bosoms. At this point, H. H. Welbert started to reach for a gun lying on a shelf under one of the desks on the south side of the room, when old Bill drawed on him and told him to get on his feet and reach for the ceiling. John M. Trew, the other bookkeeper, sitting at a desk in the rear of the room, was told to get on his feet and reach for the skies, also.

When they had got all the greenbacks they could find tucked in their shirts, they tried the rear door of the bank and found it locked, so kicked it in and went through it into the W. R. Robertson law office. W. R. had seen what was going on through a crack in the door, and took the precaution of closing and locking it. He couldn't get away because he could see Tom and the horses out the back door, through the screen, as he had the door open for air. They just kicked the door open and told W. R., who was hunched down behind his desk, to reach, and W. R. said later, "You bet I did; I was plenty willing to comply with their orders." When they tried to go out the screen door, they tried to push it out, and it wouldn't open that way, so they just busted through it.

When they got to the alley, they found that their horses were there, with the reins looped over the corner post of the coal bin, but Tom had jumped on his horse and was long gone. They mounted, Fred getting away first, and rode north toward Third Steeet, with Fred in the lead on a buckskin colored horse.* As he came out of the alley onto Third Street, W. Ray Simpson, who had run over from his hardware store, beaded down with his gun on Fred, and let him have it in the left temple. Simpson then jacked in another shell, and running a few steps east on Third where he could get a better shot at Billy, beaded on the left side of the back of his head, lifted off his hat and the entire top of his head.

Billy's body dropped in the east side of the alley, just

---

* This was a roan horse, a big gelding called Suzy that had made the trip to Oregon and back with the McCartys. He had been brought into the country from Kentucky by a couple of fellows, and traded to Maxwells at La Sal.

behind Bailey's cow barn; Fred's torso remained seated in the saddle until his horse turned west on Second Street at Hammond's barn, where it fell to the ground against the Hammond fence. The horse then turned south on Main to where, in front of Griswold's Second Hand Store, a smart aleck shot the horse back of the front legs, through the lungs. It continued south on Main Street to the Post Office hitch rack where other horses were tied, and stood among them until it fell to the ground and died in a pool of its own blood.

I was doing what I did about nine-tenths of my waking hours: bathing prints on the east porch of the shop. When Billy's torso dropped to the ground, I hurried out of our back gate and over to the body, and saw that he was dead. There were some men coming from the blacksmith shop, and I sure wanted to stay, but I was afraid my brother or the Old Man would show up and find me not bathing prints and tan my hide, so I hurried back to my job.

LEFT: Billy McCarty, shot dead during the Delta Bank robbery, was propped up with boards under his arms (see picture) so that he could be photographed.

—PHOTO COURTESY OF BENJAMIN LAYCOCK, DELTA, COLORADO

RIGHT: Fred McCarty, photographed after being shot during the Delta Bank robbery.

—PHOTO COURTESY OF BENJAMIN LAYCOCK, DELTA, COLORADO

Henry came out of the gallery on his way to the excitement, and as he went past, told me the prints were good enough. He set the basin back inside the door, and we went down to the Hammond barn and viewed the corpse of Fred McCarty.

The fellows had figured that someone should go after the coroner, and Henry suggested they send the kid, meaning me. So I was dispatched to get Warren Brown, who lived south of the Uncompahgre bridge. I ran as fast as I could to the house, and Mrs. Brown told me he was working in the garden, up on the hill. I went up there and, when I could get breath enough, told him that three men had been killed.

He came to town promptly to arrange for a coroner's jury and an inquest. The bodies were taken to the Gale Undertaking Parlors, about where Penny's store now stands. This wasn't a place like the funeral parlors are today. It was just a shed—and Gale also sold cement and lumber, and furniture, and was also a building contractor in the usual early day line-up.

The next morning we decided to take pictures of the two outlaws, and my brother and I went down to Gale's. Gale was there and helped us carry the bodies out to the south side of the building and stack them up against the building for pictures.

Now, Fred had stiffened up pretty good during the night, and we stood him up against the building and got his picture right away. But the old man hadn't "set up" a bit, he was as limp as a wet sack, and we had a heck of a time to get him up against the building. Finally we put boards under his arms, and Gale and I held him until just as Henry was ready to take the picture. He looked like hell with the whole top of his head shot off, so Gale rustled around and got a hat to set on his head. We let go of him, jumped back out of the way, Henry snapped the picture, and we grabbed him before he toppled over on the ground.

We then returned the bodies to the mortuary, where at 10 o'clock September 8 (and not the 7th as the reports on file show) Coroner Brown called his witnesses into session and the inquest was held, showing that the two outlaws came to their deaths from gunshot wounds at the hands of one W. Ray Simpson. However, juryman A. R. King objected to my testifying for the fact that I was a minor. Coroner Brown overruled the objection, and my testimony was taken, but present findings on file carry no record of any testimony of mine.

The money was taken from the shirt bosoms of the two robbers, and restored to Daniel S. Baldwin, president of the bank.

Andrew Blachly left a family of eight boys, and a small ranch on Garnet Mesa. Mrs. Blachly raised the family, giving piano lessons to augment their income. Baldwin might have helped out a little, but there was no provision in those days for caring for the family of a man killed in the line of duty.

After Tom McCarty made his getaway on the afternoon of the robbery, he turned north, and crossed the Delta bridge, and went on west to West Gulch. He turned south down the Gulch to Dominguez Switch, and on to an island in the Gunnison River, where they had left fresh horses. He changed horses there, and forded to the south bank, and proceeded up the Dominguez Creek, disappearing over the ridge into the Sinbad area.

Thus ended Mr. Laycock's graphic narrative of the Delta Bank robbery as seen through the eyes of a twelve-year-old boy, and also from him the pictures of the two outlaws were obtained, bearing out his story. The picture of Tom McCarty came from Mr. Laycock, as well as the one of Simpson. This picture of Tom McCarty has been printed, but Mr. Laycock gave me the original.

The Delta robbery finished the McCartys, with the killing of two of them and the outlawing of Tom. Never again did he ride with the Wild Bunch; in fact, there is no reason to believe he ever saw Butch Cassidy or Elzy Lay again.

The Wild Bunch was getting more active at this time, reaching their prime in the next five or six years. Although Butch Cassidy is given most of the attention today, Lay was undoubtedly the brains of the combination, and to him must go credit for the daring planning and aggressiveness of the loosely knit band of outlaws of the Old West.

ELZY LAY

Elzy Lay was born in Iowa, near Red Oak, son of James Landis and Mary Jane Ballew Lay. The family moved to Wray, Colorado, when he was small. The name is pronounced Elza, and is often spelled that way, but records of the family in the possession of his daughter, Mrs. J. T. Murdock, Heber City, Utah, spell it with a "y" and there is no indication that it was a nickname, or that it was a diminutive.

Moving to Wray also was the Maginnis family, and Elzy and Billy Maginnis were inseparables as boys, getting into and out of the usual scrapes of farm boys on the frontier. When they were in their late teens, Elzy kept hearing of the Wild West, and wanted to go and try his luck as, at least, cowboy and adventurer.

He and Billy planned to ride to western Colorado where, somewhere in the Brown's Hole country, Elzy thought they might run into some excitement. They had put their outfits together, but at the last minute Billy couldn't make the break. Elzy left, while Billy stayed home, went to school, became Colorado State Treasurer and Auditor. The

two never met again, but Elzy took the name William (or
Mac) Maginnis pretty consistently, and made the name
somewhat more glamorous than its rightful owner ever
did.

While in the Old Ashley Valley, in Uintah County, Utah,
Lay went one day to the home of Albert Davis, with whom
he had been working, putting up hay. When he came into
the house, Albert's sister, Maude, took one look at him and
in her words sixty years later, "knew he was the man for
me; it was love at first sight for both of us."

Elzy Lay would have been the dream man for any girl.
He was tall, slender, dark complexioned, with beautiful
dark eyes, and possessed of an outstanding gracefulness
in a land where riding and outdoor activity made every
man a demigod. Extremely intelligent, he radiated charm,
and everyone mentions his courtly manner and air of easy
leadership. He was called the educated outlaw, and some
writers even build him a Boston background.

Although Butch Cassidy is given the credit for leadership of the Wild Bunch, oldtimers maintain that Lay was
actually the brains of the group, and Butch followed his
lead. The two men were so close, however, it is difficult to
tell who made the decisions. Other men joined them for a
time, but Lay and Butch were together for most of their
outlaw careers, parting only when Lay (against Butch's
advice) participated in the holdup of the Colorado Southern with Ketchum.

Ann Bassett, cattle queen of Brown's Hole, mentions
how good looking and personable Lay was. At that time
he was using his own name. Ann tells in the *Colorado His-
torical Journal* how she, together with Maude and a minister, crossed Green River on a dark night in late fall and
met Lay on a mountain side by prearrangement, where
the minister joined him and Maude in marriage. Ann then
guided the man of the cloth back to the river, and helped
him return to civilization, while Lay and Maude left on a
horseback honeymoon.

The next glimpse we have of Maude is in the fall of 1896.
At a dance in Green River, Jim McPherson met a girl
who told him she wanted some information. Evidently
someone had pointed him out to her as being able to sup-

LEFT: Elzy Lay, as he looked about the time he and Maude Davis were married, about 1896.

RIGHT: Maude Davis, sometime after she and Elzy Lay were married, probably photographed in 1899 or 1900.

ply the answers to some questions. Jim told her to fire away. She wanted to know how long she might have to wait for a wagon to take her out to the Roost, that she had been told to come to Green River and wait. Jim assured her everything would be all right, the wagon would be along, not to get impatient.

And the wagon did come in the next day or so, driven by Blue John, who loaded it to the wagon-bows with groceries and ammunition, and they set out for the Roost. Not many people knew he had a passenger; the fact was not advertised.

After a slow trip across the desert, which the girl thoroughly enjoyed, stopping at San Rafael, Cottonwood, North Springs, they pulled up at last on the ridge overlooking Roost Flats. The girl asked Blue John how much farther it was, and he pointed to the little pink pinnacle, Runt's Knob, far across the graceful swales and undulating ridges of Roost Flats, and told her that the pack train would meet them there. The wagon lumbered slowly across the miles and drew up in a long narrow park in the cedars, where some horses grazed.

Elzy Lay and another fellow got up from under a tree, where they had been waiting. After greetings were exchanged, they caught the packhorses and started sorting out loads. Immediately needed supplies were chosen and loaded, and the heavily laden pack string, with the four riders, set off on Badman Trail into Horseshoe Canyon. Traveling down the canyon a short distance, they climbed out on the eastern rim into the Upper Pasture. Here in the thick cedars on the canyon rim, with only the one trail up to it, a permanent camp had been established. There were two large tents for the group, and a smaller tent to which Elzy led Maude.

A few days later another pack string of supplies jingled down the canyon and up the trail, and another girl dismounted. A small tent was unloaded for her, and she and Butch set up housekeeping. Both couples ate with the men, but spent most of their time in their tents, or taking walks together among the cedars on the sandy ridges.

The identity of this other girl was for a long time a mystery. Many people told me in all seriousness it was Sadie Moran, Jack Moran's daughter—that it was Rose Maguire—also, that Nancy Ingalls claimed the honor. Finally, in 1970, Harry Longabaugh's son stated it was Etta Place, and Marvel Lay Murdock corroborated the fact, saying her mother, Maude Davis Lay, loved and admired Etta Place, stating she was the most beautiful woman she had ever seen.

Elzy Lay's wife was very well known to several men, who told me they had seen her there that winter. But none of them knew the other girl for sure. A winter spent with Elzy Lay or Butch Cassidy surely would not have damaged a girl's reputation in my opinion—I *envy* her!

While the girls killed time, the men were plenty busy. They had collected and were busy graining * and train-

---

* To put a really fine finish on a horse, oats (about 1 to 2 gallons) were fed him twice a day. Together with the fine nutritious desert grasses, this put a real finish on him, especially if he received a good hard workout each day.

ing four horses for the Castle Gate payroll holdup they were planning. Kid was a big brown horse from the Uintah Basin, and they had given Jack Moore the money to buy Gray Eagle from the Swaseys in Emery County. Joe Walker had stolen the sorrel horse from the Whitmores, but it turned out they used a little bay horse belonging to Jack Moran in the actual holdup. The bay mare, Babe, was apparently well known, but her background has not been established.

Blue John took the girls back to civilization in March, about a month before the Castle Gate holdup.

A few months after the holdup, Elzy went back to Ashley Valley to get Maude, but she had seen enough and heard enough of the life of an outlaw and wanted him to settle down and quit his wild ways. He couldn't see it. There was still a lot more country to see, many more wild rides to make, and much excitement to life as he wanted to live it. After a long talk, they decided there could be no future for them together and Lay mounted his horse and rode away.

Maude, grief stricken, obtained a divorce and turned to making a life for herself and her little daughter, Marvel, who was born prematurely that August. After a while Maude married Orrin Curry—no relation to the outlaw Currys—and Marvel grew up under that name until she was fourteen years old. In that year, 1911, she was graduated from the eighth grade, and her father came to her graduation exercises. She met him a year or two later, and from then until his death she maintained a close contact with him and spent a great deal of time with him and his family.

When Maude declined to live a married life on the dodge, Elzy returned to Brown's Park, where Butch was waiting for him. Together they bought a white-topped buggy in which to haul their camp, hired a driver and started to Arizona with a string of horses.

Passing through Thompson Springs, Utah, the outfit stopped, and Butch came into Ballard Brothers Store to buy supplies and ask permission to water their horses. Bud Milton was running the store and told them to go ahead, the troughs were in the corral. Milton was a fine horseman, ran a string of race horses throughout the West for several years a few years after this episode, and he couldn't help noticing these outstanding horses. He also noted that his attention was not welcome, so he didn't venture out of the store. However, he strongly suspected who his customers were, and was told a few days later, he had been right.

At Alma, New Mexico, Captain French, an Irish nobleman, who was running the WS Cattle outfit for an English concern, hired the two competent looking men in the summer of 1897. In his *Recollections of a Western Ranchman,* written during and after his sojourn at the main ranch at Alma, he tells how they solved his problems of local cattle rustling quickly and thoroughly.

Throughout the West, cattle rustling from the big outfits was no small problem, it is said that most of them were finally put out of business by this local thievery. After Butch and the Wild Bunch came to work for the WS, all this ceased, and the cows that the boys ran onto carrying dubious brands were promptly rebranded for the outfit. While French was delighted to have the company profiting by these activities, he was apprehensive that there might be some outcry from the local "petty larceny" crowd, as Butch and Lay dubbed them, which could well land the WS in a lawsuit. There was never a peep, and French marveled, not knowing that throughout the ranges, the reputation of the Wild Bunch was such that petty thieves backed off immediately, knowing those boys played for keeps.

At the time, the WS was moving its operations into eastern New Mexico, where it had bought ranches. French put Butch in charge of the trail herds from Alma across the mountains and the San Augustin Plains into Magdalena, the rail head. Lay went along, also, starting out with ten or twelve head of raw broncs on a cattle drive, and by the time the herd was on the cars at Magdalena, he had a saddle string of well-broken horses. This was a big advantage to the outfit, as they needed plenty of well-broken saddle horses in their operations in the rough ranges of western New Mexico.

While the outfit was in town, there were never any

drunken brawls or shooting up the town. The WS at this time carried a reputation of having the best behaved cattle crews in the country. French marveled at that, too, mentioning that, although he would be perturbed when some really outstanding "hand" would want to leave, Butch didn't mind and seemed to be able to command an almost unlimited force of superb cowboys; he was never short-handed. French strongly suspected who Butch and Lay were, but he had never had it so good, and he didn't try to find out how many of his crew belonged to the Wild Bunch—he didn't even care.

Finally Lay and Butch came to French and said that Lay would like to quit; most of the horses had been broken and he didn't want to do other work. French was reluctant to have him go, but he did see the reason in it. Lay offered to oversee the trainload of cattle to Springer, as he was headed for Colorado and that would put him that far on his way. He made the same deal for "Red," one of the lesser cow hands who was going with him.

This was all right with French, but he mentions that Butch and Lay seemed to be in some sort of argument, and he deduced it was over this Red. However, the disagreement went much deeper than that; Lay wanted Butch to join him and the Ketchums in a train robbery. Butch despised the Ketchums, and he was trying to talk Elzy out of going with them. However, Lay persisted, since they were trying to get together money enough to "retire" to South America, and left with the cattle.

Sam Ketchum, Elzy Lay and Kid Curry (who had been using the name Tom Capehart at the WS) hit the Colorado & Southern at Folsom, some seventy miles east of Springer, New Mexico. The express car was moved away from the rest of the train, and the safe blown open, disgorging some $30,000 for the three robbers. Nobody was hurt, and the three train robbers left, going up Cimarron Canyon, where they camped at Turkey Creek.

A posse followed them under Sheriff Farr of Trinidad, Colorado. They came upon the camp early in the morning, and when Elzy Lay started toward the creek with his canteen opened fire on him. Wounded, he rolled into an arroyo, and the battle was joined. Sam Ketchum was wounded in the arm, which left the defense of the camp to Kid Curry, one of the most expert with a gun and the coolest of the Wild Bunch. That night, Tom Smith, a cowpuncher from Trinidad, was there with a lantern looking around, trying to find tracks at night. He straightened up, Kid Curry shot and Tom Smith was dead before he hit the ground.

The next morning, three of the posse had been killed, including Sheriff Farr, and one badly wounded. And the outlaws had disappeared, although it was known two of them were wounded. Not long after, Sam Ketchum was apprehended and taken to prison, suffering from a gunshot wound in his arm. He died a few days later of blood poisoning.

No trace could be found of the other two, although it was common knowledge that one of them, a certain Mac who had worked for the WS outfit was badly wounded.

About a month later, Jim Lowe (Butch Cassidy) came in from the Horse Camp, about twenty miles out in the mountains, to talk to Captain French. He said that Mac had been taken prisoner, and French asked him how he knew about it. He said that Tom Capehart had ridden in the night before, both he and his horse in bad shape, and Tom had changed mounts and ridden out to the Horse Camp.

Tom Capehart told French that he and Lay had ridden down into Lincoln County, some 300 miles from the scene of the robbery, where they intended to get jobs on a ranch somewhere. Lay was badly wounded, shot through the body twice, and had not been able to take care of his wounds. However, no complications had developed and he was healing slowly.

Tom had tried to get a job, but had been unable to, so they decided to hit across the state to the WS, and Tom went to town for supplies and ammunition for the eight- or ten-day trip. They were to meet at a cabin near a spring where they had been getting water while Lay hid out in the hills. Although Lay had been recognized, Kid Curry never was, and he was able to move around a little.

Lay came to the cabin first. A posse out after some horse thieves had arrived at the cabin shortly after dawn and, taking the owner prisoner, were hiding in the cabin lying in wait for the horse thieves. When Lay came in, they told him to put up his hands, and of course he thought they were taking him for the train robbery. He had only one bullet in his sixshooter, so he shot one man through the wrist, then went at them with his fists. They had to beat him unconscious to subdue him, then they found by his bloody shirt and his partly healed wounds that they had bagged a much bigger quarry than a horse thief, and took him to town. He was lodged in the Colfax County jail at Raton, and held for trial as a train robber.

French appeared at his trial and attested to his good character, but he was sentenced to life imprisonment and was taken to the New Mexico Territorial Prison at Sante Fe on October 10, 1899.

There was never anything commonplace or mediocre about Elzy Lay; he stood out as much in prison as he had on the range—maybe even more so. The warden immediately chose him to take care of his team when he went into Santa Fe, and he made several trips a week into the capital city.

Returning one time, they found that the lifers of the prison had rioted and taken the wife and daughters of the warden as hostages. Lay volunteered to talk to the rioters, and because they knew him, liked and trusted him he was able to quell the riot and reclaim the hostages. It is thought that as a result of this, he received a pardon from Governor Otero on January 10, 1906.

Another story is that he wouldn't tell where the loot from the train was buried, and he was released in the hope he would lead the authorities to it. He knew the loot was long gone, and we will hear more of that later.

Returning to Alma, he stayed around there for several months, then rode north to Baggs, Wyoming, where he either bought or worked in a saloon. He had been committed to prison under the name of William Maginnis, alias Elzy Lay, and when he returned to Baggs, he was still using the name Maginnis, and everyone called him

Mac. He courted and married Mary Calvert, daughter of one of the leading ranch families in southern Wyoming, who insisted he change back to his own name, and he never used the name Maginnis again.

An oil geologist from New York came into the area to do some oil exploration work and asked a banker by the name of Maupin at Rawlins if he could recommend someone to guide him, someone of a little intelligence, who would be able to handle horses and be a companion for the summer. Maupin told him about Lay and gave him the background, which was interesting to the Eastern man, but not particularly prejudicial.

After Lay had worked for him for a month or so, the geologist wrote Maupin thanking him for recommending a man of Lay's caliber for the job. He had found him intelligent and with a great interest in geology and the ability to apply his knowledge. When the geologist returned to New York, he sent Lay books on geology, particularly pertaining to oil-bearing formations, and Lay studied them and applied the information. He chose a location near Baggs, and interested his friends into going into the endeavor with him, and brought in a rig to drill a well. The driller wanted to drill another place, but Lay insisted he knew what he was doing.

The equipment was not very good, and they were hopelessly underfinanced, so the hole had to be abandoned. Lay had put in all the money he had and had induced his friends to advance considerable funds, so that when the project folded, he was completely defeated and left the country. Several months later, Mary found him in southern California and took the two children down and joined him there. She nursed him back to health, and he spent the rest of his working years as head watermaster, manthe main headgate of the Imperial Valley Irrigation system.

He never went back to Baggs to live, nor did he keep up assessment work on the oil claims. A few years later the Mountain Fuel and Supply Company put down a well on the location where he had failed to find oil, and brought in the Hiawatha oil field, from which Ogden and Salt Lake City receive their supply of natural gas today.

On his first trip to visit Marvel at Ashley Valley in Utah, he didn't bring his wife. But later they picked her up and made a trip east to visit his parents and sister.

Marvel remembers what an expert shot her father was. He could throw a can into the air and empty his gun, twirling it between shots, and keep the can in the air, hitting it with every shot.

On his next visit after the trip east, Marvel was living at Heber City, high in the Wasatch Mountains. Lay suffered a heart attack and had to leave. He returned to his job in California, at Calexico, where he and Mary had established their home. She always came with him to see Marvel, and the two women loved each other dearly.

After Lay retired, he moved his family to Los Angeles, where he died November 10, 1934, and was buried at Forest Lawn Cemetery, using his own name, Elzy Lay. This name stood for fearlessness, likeableness and intelligence among an entire generation of range riders and ranchers of the West. These men credited him with the brains of the Lay-Cassidy partnership, but Butch was quite a jasper in his own right and carried his own legend.

BUTCH CASSIDY

Robert LeRoy Parker came from pioneer Mormon stock. His father, Maximillian Parker, was nine years old when the family was converted in England, and shipped out to join the "Saints" in Utah. His mother, Ann Gillies, was a Scottish lassie, converted also in her homeland.

In the early days of the Church of Jesus Christ of Latter Day Saints, missionaries sent to northern Europe and England made a strong effort to convert artisans and craftsmen. It was no accident that when the church leaders sent out colonies to establish settlements in their new Zion, there were blacksmiths, weavers, tinsmiths, brickmakers and carpenters, as well as farmers and stockmen, and that the groups could sustain themselves in an often unfriendly land.

Robert LeRoy's grandfather, Robert Parker, was a weaver in Preston, England. He was educated and successful. He always invited the Mormon Elders to stay at his home, and was soon converted to the new faith by missionaries who were preaching an earthly land of opportunity,

This photograph, usually palmed off on the unsuspecting as picturing Butch Cassidy, is actually Mike Steele, who grew up in and around Wayne County.

—PHOTO COURTESY OF CASS MULFORD, TORREY, UTAH

as well as a new religion. To the men of limited opportunities in England, this sounded most promising.

Robert sold his home and set out with his family for the new Zion early in the spring of 1856. Besides their son Maximillian, the Parkers had a son Dan about five, a daughter about seven and a baby girl. They came with the Second Handcart Company on the *Enoch Train* under McArthur, and after a seven-week ocean voyage, went by train to Iowa City, where they started out for Utah, more than 1,000 miles away, pushing a handcart.

When the floods of immigrants converted by the missionaries, hit the western outposts of American settlement, the Mormon leaders were unable to cope with the situation. Later, wagon trains were sent back from Utah to bring in the people, but some of the earlier ones were, in the desperation of the Church leaders to get them to Utah, organized into handcart companies.

Two-wheeled carts were hurriedly knocked together, and each family piled its belongings into the cart and set out, pulling and pushing, for the Land of Promise. A few oxcarts and wagons with teams hauled some provisions, but each family was responsible for transporting a good share of the food and all its personal effects.

The first group left early in the spring, and came through in pretty good shape, men, women and children walking all the way. The Parkers were in the Second Company, arriving in Salt Lake City in September. The Gillies family came in a wagon train late that year, arriving in Utah probably in December, following the tragic Fifth Handcart party under Martin. They settled in Woods Cross,

The old Parker home three miles south of Circleville, Utah, just over the line of Garfield County. The family was living here when Robert LeRoy Parker left in 1884 to being his outlaw life and become known later on as Butch Cassidy.

—PHOTOGRAPHED IN 1969 BY PARKER HAMILTON

and the Parkers moved to American Fork, where Robert Parker taught school. The next spring both families were called by the Church leaders to move to Beaver, Robert Gillies to help build the houses of the new community as he was a carpenter and cabinet maker, and Robert Parker to help set up a woolen mill in Beaver.

A few years later Parker was called to Washington, Utah, where the mild climate of Utah's "Dixie" produced cotton and mulberry trees upon which silk worms were being nourished. He was to set up a cotton mill, which would also take care of the silk production. After the dream of a cotton empire faded because it cost three times as much to raise cotton and process it as to ship the cloth in, Parker was put in charge of the co-op store, which had run into difficulties. He was an organizer and businessman, and soon had the store running profitably.

When the other Parkers left Beaver, Maximillian remained, marrying Ann Gillies on her eighteenth birthday. They lived in Beaver for a few years, where their first son, Robert LeRoy, was born on April 13, 1866. When he was about 12, and there were several other children in the family, the Parkers moved to Circleville.

Things were going rather well for the young couple. They had several head of cattle and had bought a ranch three miles south of Circleville. But after the terrible winter of 1878-79, only one cow remained. This was a crippling blow and for a few years the family was close to read hardship, as were many of their neighbors. Maximillian went to Silver Reef to cut timbers for the mines, and after a year or two, when they had accumulated a few milk cows, Ann moved out to the Marshall ranch where she made butter and cheese for family use and some to sell.

Robert LeRoy was about fifteen when she moved to the Marshall ranch, and he was a real help. The last couple of years out there, a tough bunch of men made the place their headquarters, with Mike Cassidy as leader. He took a shine to the manly, engaging Robert, gave him a gun and a saddle and established himself in the eyes of the teen-age lad as a real hero. Ann disapproved highly of this association; she tried to keep Robert away from the men, and finally moved into town in the fall. But the damage had been done, Robert never lived under her roof again, and in the spring of 1884 he struck out for himself. Maximillian had given up his job by that time, and the fortunes of the family had mended somewhat. They were then, and always remained, one of the leading stockgrowing families of the area, interested always in fine horses.

Mike Cassidy had left the country, things having become a little hot for him. The men who had been in his gang, local ranchers for the most part, rounded up a bunch of the best saddle horses on the range and sent Robert LeRoy to Telluride with them. He made delivery, the men showed up long enough to collect the proceeds and then bade him *adios* and returned to Utah.*

Robert had had enough of Utah. He was husky and competent and felt he could sell his talents better at Telluride. He spent a couple of years packing ore down the mountain from the mine to the mill, and then went to the Hole-in-the-Wall country of Wyoming, where he met some of the men (Longabaugh, for one) who later became the Wild Bunch.

He had returned to Telluride when Matt Warner and Tom McCarty came along racing the mare Betty, and he joined them. After the Telluride bank job, he set out for Wyoming again, landing in Rock Springs. He was then using the name George Cassidy and, as the only job he could get was working in a butcher shop, he was soon called "Butch" which fitted euphonically to Cassidy.

The butcher shop didn't claim Butch for long; he was always an outdoor man and soon was riding the range again. One of his fellow riders, Harry Bennett, later moved to Utah and became a good friend of my father's. I had heard for years that he knew Butch well, but since he never mentioned it, I was afraid to, but men kept telling me he had ridden closely with the Wild Bunch (although he was never at any time or in any sense one of them), and knew plenty.

---

* This is the story told to me by the Parkers, and the one generally believed. It is my understanding that a different reason for his leaving home has later come to light.

The Bennetts had moved to Ogden, Utah, before I got up nerve enough to ask him about it. Making a special trip there to see what Harry would say, I found him most cooperative and spent one wonderful fall day listening to stories I could have found in no other way. Two things that I did not accept then were confirmed by later material: One was that a bay mare and not the Moran horse, as I had been told, was used in the Castle Gate holdup, and the other, and far more important one, was that Butch had come back to the West from South America.

Butch and Harry had ridden together, but Butch was already "a little on the rustle." The ranch on which they both worked was the 4H outfit, fourteen miles east of Buffalo, Wyoming, owned by W. H. Howland. Butch had worked, too, for the Pitchfork outfit in 1890–91 in the Big Horn Basin.

Most of the big outfits in Wyoming at the time were owned by Eastern men, who had put up the money to buy the stock, but hired local foremen and hands. These included the Half-Circle Block, called the Bay State outfit from Boston, on the west side of the Big Horn Mountain; the FK outfit a few miles north of the Pitchfork; 76 spread on the north fork of Powder River, which Fruen owned and managed; the TA-connected on Crazy Woman Creek; the CY on down Flat River, run by Mike Shaughnessy, and owned by J. M. Carey, the first elected senator from Wyoming; and the Bar FS on the Bellefourche River, owned by E. W. Whitcomb. Flat Nose George worked for the Bar FS, and others of the future Wild Bunch were riding the range in and around this locality—the Logans, Kid Curry, Longabaugh (the Sundance Kid) and most of the others who became so well known later in Utah.

These outfits, or rather their foremen, looked on the small ranch Butch and Al Hainer were starting with some suspicion. Harry said Butch got into trouble over a horse that Billy Nutcher stole and sold to him for $5.00. This was a frame-up to get rid of Butch and Hainer, because the ranchers believed them far too capable with a long loop. When Claverly, the deputy, made a raid on the camp where Butch and Hainer had their headquarters, they naturally put up a battle, but were taken anyway. This jibes with material found at the Utah Historical Society in *Morals, Colorado Project:*

> He and Al Hainer were partners on a small homestead in Wyoming. They were merely average by standards of the day. They drank, gambled, and rode the range from around Lander on to Lost Cabin and Owl Creek country. Soon they sold out and vanished. In a short while they appeared in Lander with a great deal of money, telling fantastic tales of having made it in Colorado, then disappeared again after whooping it up awhile in Fremont County's new capital.
>
> The spring of '94 a Fremont County deputy made a quiet trip. He was an excellent man, selected to strike a blow at horse thieves who were making life a nightmare for the ranchers of the section.
>
> The deputy, Claverly, came back with a number of stolen horses and (not taken without violence) two prisoners, well known in Lander. Butch Cassidy was the name George Parker had taken. Perhaps it was because his family in the Sevier Valley of Utah was a respectable family (a sister later became postmistress at Circleville).*
>
> When Claverly and his deputy came upon their men in camp below Green River, the typical bravery of the desperado of that period was shown in Cassidy's resistance. Al Hainer (Cassidy's partner) immediately surrendered, but Cassidy himself fought savagely, suffering a pistol slug through his scalp and was subdued only when the barrel of Claverly's pistol crashed into and fractured his jaw.
>
> Sentiment was mixed in Lander, as it was all over the West at that time in such cases. Cassidy was a friendly, likeable man. The town had known him well, had liked him well, and he had done little more than steal a few horses.

---

* In my notes, when they were read by two of Butch's sisters, Jen Penaluna and Lula Betenson, in 1954, Jen wrote NO! above this parenthetical comment. Butch's grandfather, Robert Parker, was postmaster at Washington, Utah, and an uncle, Dan Gillies, had been postmaster at Circleville, but none of the immediate family had held that position.

But, in spite of the few horses, he was convicted and sentenced to two years in the Laramie Penitentiary. Hainer,
who surrendered, was acquitted. These circumstances sent
Cassidy to the penitentiary for a light sentence. A shift in
the circumstances of his capture and he might have been
dangling from a cottonwood tree at the end of a tightly
noosed lariat.

In January, 1896, Governor Richards pardoned Cassidy . . .

Butch began serving his sentence July 15, 1894, and
was given the number 184. The story is widely told that
Governor Richards pardoned him if he would promise not
to bother Wyoming again, but I have never corroborated
that. It strikes me that he might have received some time
off for good behavior, and that he might have served out
his entire sentence, being released a few months ahead of
time.

Butch Cassidy emerged from the Wyoming Penitentiary January 16, 1896, feeling an outlaw. He set out for
Brown's Park to recruit the Wild Bunch, so-called because
they raised such hell when they came to town to celebrate
in Baggs, Vernal or other frontier towns. Saloon keepers
called them "that wild bunch from Brown's Park" and let
them shoot up the place as much as they pleased, well
knowing that they would come back and pay for all damage. It is said that bullet holes in the bar were worth $1
each, and the rest of the damage was always settled for
generously. Butch had planned to call the gang he was
going to organize the *Train Robbers Syndicate*, but history has sort of bypassed that title for the more descrip-
tive "Wild Bunch."

The first test of his leadership came in August, when
one of their gang, Matt Warner, got into trouble over killing the two men as told in Chapter VI. Butch and his first
lieutenant, Lay, held up the Montpelier Bank (so Matt
says) to obtain money to hire Douglas A. Preston to defend Matt. Bob (or Bub) Meeks went along to hold the
horses, and spent several years in jail after he was ap-

prehended by the law and identified by one of the employees of the bank.

The next robbery was the holdup at Castle Gate of the Pleasant Valley Coal Company payroll, covered in Chapter 17. After that, things were so hot in Utah, Wyoming, Idaho and the other states of the Northwest, that Butch and Lay drifted into New Mexico, hiring on with the WS Cattle Company at Alma in the summer of 1897. Butch took the name of Jim Lowe, and Lay became known as William Maginnis, with the nickname of Mac.

Shortly after Lay entered the New Mexico Territorial Prison in October, 1899, a detective from the Pinkerton's Detective Agency came to Captain French, manager of the WS, looking for the man who had passed some bills from the Wilcox holdup. He asked French if he recognized any of three men in a faded picture. French said that one of the men was Lowe and another was Tom Capehart. The detective then said Lowe was Butch Cassidy, wanted throughout the West as being the leader of the Wild Bunch. Capehart was identified by French, but the Pinkerton detective did not say who he actually was. In all truth, he might have been either Kid Curry or the Sundance Kid (Longabaugh); however, it is generally conceded that it was Kid Curry at the Colorado & Southern holdup at Folson, and if so, then the other man whom French identified as Tom Capehart was Kid Curry. When French asked the detective if he was going to arrest Lowe, he laughed and said it would take a regiment to arrest him in that locality. He was interested only in the man who had passed the unsigned currency.

When Lowe returned from town, French told him of the visit, and Lowe laughed and said he and Tom had bought the man a drink, suspecting who he was.

French had no intention of firing the best trail boss he had ever seen, but things worked out so that he lost Lowe, anyway. French's foreman wanted to quit and suggested that Butch be put in that position. French called Butch into the office, and in the discussion that followed, Butch was made to see that French could not accord him that

authority in view of his past record. This must have been
a bitter blow to Butch—to see a career in the work he
knew go down the drain because he was burdened with a
past he regretted.

He quit soon after, and the next time French heard
about him (other than to assure an Arizona deputy sheriff
that Butch was honorably possessed of his saddle horses)
was from a survey outfit the next spring that was survey-
ing the Maxwell Land Grant in eastern New Mexico. At
least French thought it was Butch and Capehart.

When Butch left the WS, he asked French for a set of
pack bags that were somewhat the product of the WS.
These bags were made by shrinking wet rawhide over a
cedar-branch frame, making durable "boxes" some 2 feet
by 16 or 18 inches deep and about 14 inches thick. These
stiff bags, unlike the soft bags used for duffle, carried supplies and utensils safely without mashing anything.

The survey crew remarked about these bags, used by
a couple of competent-looking cowboys, who went through
northeastern New Mexico. French concluded it was Butch
and Capehart picking up the loot from the Folsom robbery.

A few months prior to this, in the early spring of 1900,
the Union Pacific got understandably uneasy and decided
it might be a good idea to get Butch on their side. He had
applied to Governor Wells of Utah, asking for some kind
of amnesty deal whereby he could "retire" without going
to the penitentiary. The Governor threw out the application when he heard that Butch was wanted in Wyoming
for murder. This was not true—Butch Cassidy never killed
a man in his whole outlaw career, he deemed it stupid and
poor planning. Attorney Powers of Salt Lake City, who
had been Butch's advocate with the Governor, then approached the Union Pacific and found them receptive to
the proposition. It would kill two birds with one stone,
eliminate his daring leadership of the Train Robbing Syndicate and also scare off fledgling outlaws. A meeting was
set up at Lost Soldier Pass, with Douglas Preston accom-
panying the railroad officials. A bad storm delayed the
party, and Butch, after waiting a day or two decided the
deal was off. He figured he was in too deep, anyway.

While the railroad officials were trying to make contact with him, the Tipton job on the Union Pacific at the westward siding roughly halfway between Rawlins and Rock Springs, at mile 740.4, on August 29, 1900, demolished his chances with them as effectively as he and the Wild Bunch demolished the baggage car. In this robbery, Laura Bullion participated, the first time a woman had been on a job. She was traveling with Ben Kilpatrick. Another oddity of this job is the fact that the railroad said they made a haul of $50.45, but Woodcock, the same messenger that the Wild Bunch had blown out of the car on the Wilcox robbery, stated later that they had made a haul of $55,000. It is speculated that the railroad was becoming alarmed that people would be afraid to ship large sums of money or other valuables if the Wild Bunch was going to pluck it out of the baggage car.

Less than a month after the Tipton job, Butch, Sundance and Bill Carver held up the bank at Winnemucca, Nevada. They were camped outside town and rode in that morning, with Carver coming across the fields. He was dressed in old clothes and carried a shabby bedroll, looking like a bum with no connection with the spruce outlaws. He was to come in and sit in the lobby, with the bed roll concealing a rifle in absolutely first-class condition and ready for use. He was insurance.

After a trip to Winnemucca to research that bank robbery, I received some pertinent information on that event from I. V. (Vic) Button of Sacramento, California, who stated on November 21, 1970:

> In the fall of the year 1900, three man camped by a haystack on the CS Ranch east of Winnemucca on the Humboldt river. This was my father's ranch and I was about ten years old. I went down every day to visit them. They had this white horse—I had never seen such a horse. He could jump over high sagebrush, willow fences or anything. I rode a different horse down every day and Butch would ride the white horse, but I could never beat the white horse. Butch said, "You like that horse? Some day he will be yours."

I became quite well acquainted with them, they were good to me and brought me candy . . . asked me many questions about the bank and about the country. I told them about Soldier's Pass, a short cut to Clover Valley.

After the robbery a posse of Jim McVey, Shorty Johnson and Burns Colwell caught up with them at Clover Valley. The robbers had just opened and closed a wire gate, and told the posse they would shoot it out with them, but the posse turned to ride back. Butch shouted, "Give the white horse to the kid at the CS Ranch!" It was at this point they were changing mounts and leaving the white horse behind. We learned later they had relay mounts set up all the way to the Idaho border.

When the posse came to Golconda I was coming out of the schoolhouse. I looked up and there was my white horse, covered with dried sweat and lather from his hard run. I jumped on him. There was a high willow fence around the schoolyard and I jumped him over the fence then took him to the creek to water.

Everyone was watching me and they asked about the robbers. I could only say, "You see what they gave me."

For a man, when he was crowded by a posse, to remember his promise to a kid—makes you think he could not have been all bad.

On December 1, 1970 he added:

You will probably notice that I named posse members other than what you have read. Sheriff McDeid did not organize the posse . . . I knew the posse members well, as they came to the school with the white horse.

I would also like to pass on another story to you that was told to me. In the 1930s when banks were in trouble, two receivers came to work in the bank at Winnemucca. One of these men and his wife went to New Mexico to the funeral of a relative of his wife.

When they returned he told me that while they were in the cemetery, one of the family introduced them to friends and mentioned they were from Winnemucca, Nevada.

A woman putting flowers on a grave next to theirs came

and said she couldn't help overhearing and this grave was
her husband, who had been one of Butch Cassidy's gang.
He had been on the Winnemucca holdup and told her about
giving the horse to the kid "Vic" and wondered if he was
still alive. She said her husband had come to New Mexico,
changed his name and lived there until his death.*

The boys went to Fort Worth, Texas, where they met
some of the rest of the Wild Bunch and put on a celebration that resulted in the famous picture of the five of them,
Butch, Fitzpatrick, Sundance, Carver and Harvey Logan.
Butch returned this picture to the bank in Winnemucca
with a note thanking them for their contribution. The picture, or rather an enlargement of it, hangs in the bank
lobby today.

The United States was getting pretty hot for the boys.
Pinkerton's detectives were becoming better organized,
and more efficient men were in the field. The old dream of
going to South America to retire looked better and better,
so after staging another train robbery at Wagner, Montana, on the Great Northern, Butch met Sundance in New
York City in the early days of 1902 to travel to the southern continent.

Sundance had Etta Place with him, and Butch looked
with much disfavor on her company. However, Sundance
was adamant, claiming that she would be handy to have
around, could ride and shoot as well as cook and keep
house. So Butch capitulated.

They took in all the sights in New York City, pretty
much as the movie *Butch Cassidy and the Sundance Kid*
showed. They landed in Buenos Aires, but soon traveled
to the interior where they settled on a ranch in Chubut
in the Andean foothills, near the border of Chile. They
bought several hundred head of cattle, some sheep and,
of course, some good horses. They bought and sold cattle,

---

* Since Bill Carver was killed in Texas, and Butch was living at
this time in Washington, this must have been the grave of Longabaugh, the Sundance Kid, and the woman might very well have been
Etta Place.

The famous Wild Bunch photograph taken in Forth Worth after
the Winnemucca Bank holdup and sent back to the bank by
Butch Cassidy with a note of thanks for the "contribution." Left
to right: William Carver and Harvey Logan, standing behind
The Sundance Kid (Harvey Longabaugh), The Tall Texan (Ben
Kilpatrick), and Butch Cassidy (Robert LeRoy Parker).

—COURTESY OF R. D. MUDGE, VICE PRESIDENT AND MANAGER, FIRST NATIONAL BANK OF
NEVADA, WINNEMUCCA, NEVADA

too, trailing their herds over the passes into Chile where
there was a good market at the mines.

They enjoyed the Chubut ranch, they kept open house,
and Etta proved her worth as the perfect hostess. In 1906
or 1907 she began suffering attacks of appendicitis and
was forced to return to the United States where she entered the hospital at Denver for an operation. Sundance
returned with her, but as soon as she was able to get
around, he went back to South America—things were not
going well down there.

The inevitable had happened: someone had recognized Butch, and was trying to find out if the rewards were still on him. As soon as Sundance returned, they sold the ranch and moved up western South America, knocking off a few trains, banks and railroads. Their only "job" in South America up to this time had been the bank they held up to get money to return to Lay for his share of the Folsom robbery.

It was always characteristic of the Wild Bunch that when they hired out to an outfit, they were loyal to the interests of their employers. Butch and Longabaugh both held jobs of great responsibility; Seibert, manager of Concordia Mines, stated that Butch handled their payrolls in the sum of six figures occasionally, and he always gave a strict accounting.

Seibert liked Butch, who was using the name of Jim Maxwell. He knew all about his employee, and they talked frankly together. Butch told him that he couldn't go straight; as long as he lived, someone would be hounding him. The best strategy was to hit hard and keep moving.

They held up only one mine payroll, that of the San Domingo mine in Peru. The company had taken the precaution of sending a dummy coach ahead of the remittance coach, and the bandits "lost out" in a holdup which would have gained them many thousands in gold if they had been successful.

An article by Arthur Chapman in the *Elks Magazine* of April, 1930, gives an account of their activities in South America, from an interview with Mr. Seibert, manager of the Concordia mines of Bolivia. Chapman quotes Seibert as saying:

> When Cassidy worked for me at the Concordia mines, where I was manager in 1908, on coming into the sitting-room he would invariably take a seat on a small sofa which was placed between two windows. This seat gave him a survey of three doors and one window. He always seemed to be cool and calculating and protected his back very well. Although he always went armed with a Frontier Model .44 Colt, this weapon was usually stuck in his trouser belt in such a way as to be inconspicuous. I never saw him

under the influence of whiskey except once and then he seemed to be very much ashamed of himself because he could not walk straight.

When our camp was visited by two embryo American bandits on horseback, horses being very rare in the high altitudes of Bolivia, Cassidy promptly approached them and told them to get out of camp. He informed them that he did not want them or any other would be bandits to cause people to get the impression that our camp was a rendezvous for outlaws. These unwelcome visitors informed Cassidy that they realized they had not done right in coming into camp mounted on horses, but as they had to have food, there was no alternative for them. I afterwards learned that Cassidy gave them one hundred dollars, with a warning never to appear in camp again.

One night at the Concordia mines, my predecessor, Mr. Glass, and I had on the office table several hundred pounds sterling in gold, which we were counting out to pay our gold payroll men, when Cassidy came in. He jokingly remarked that it was the easiest money he had ever seen, but we continued our work and he finally asked us if we would give him the gold in exchange for paper currency. We told him we would gladly accommodate him but we would have to fulfill our obligations to certain of our men and pay them in actual gold. Cassidy then volunteered to see these men and get their consent to the exchange. This he did within an hour or two, and when he came back we made the exchange, much as we disliked being parties to such a transaction.

After the Aramayo payroll holdup in Bolivia in 1909, there was considerable concern about Butch and Sundance, and the United States was being importuned to do something about her Wild Bunch. Pinkertons sent a man down to apprehend Butch and Sundance.

Early in the spring two men rode into San Vicente asking for lodging at the police station. Throwing off their packs in a corner of the courtyard they went across to the row of adobe huts and ordered food and liquor. A native youth looked at their pack string and recognized a mule taken from a friend of his in the Aramayo holdup. He reported this to the police, who called in a troop of soldiers camped outside of town. After surrounding the compound, the soldiers called on the men to surrender, but one of them broke across the compound for the rifles, left in the packs. He got the guns, and was on his way back when the soldiers caught him with a barrage and he fell. The other bandit ran out, and although he was wounded, he managed to drag his partner and the guns into the hut.

The soldiers rushed the hut, and one was killed and several wounded. The resultant siege lasted until after nightfall.

Up to this point the story is told the same way; but from here on there are two—no, *three!*—endings. Number One from the article by Chapman in the *Elks Magazine* is:

> The battle was settled into a seige. Night came on, and men fired at the red flashes from weapons. There were spaces of increasing length between Cassidy's shots. He had only a few cartridges left. Longabaugh's cartridge belt was empty. So was the dead Bolivian captain's.
>
> The soldiers, about 9 or 10 o'clock in the evening, heard two shots fired in the bullet riddled station. Then no more shots came. Perhaps it was a ruse to lure them into the patio within range of these deadly revolvers. The soldiers kept on firing all through the night and during the next morning.
>
> About noon an officer and a detachment of soldiers rushed through the patio and into the station. They found Longabaugh and Cassidy dead. Cassidy had fired a bullet into Longabaugh's head, and had used his last cartridge to kill himself.

After Butch Cassidy returned to the United States, he visited Lander, Wyoming, and told Ed Farlow the following, as reported in *The Wyoming State Journal* of Tuesday, July 2, 1957, by Bill Marion:

TOOK UNIFORM

The story we got was that during the fight Butch was able to drag one of the dead rurales in the station, stripped him of his uniform, put the uniform on himself and his clothes on the dead rurale.

He made his way to the river and floated down it until he came to a Bolivian Indian camp. A squaw took care of him until he was able to travel.

He took off his clothes and showed Farlow the numerous bullet wounds and scars he got in that last desperate fight.

The third version is sort of a bonus. In 1970 after the movie *Butch Cassidy and the Snndance Kid* came out, a man showed up in Ogden, Utah, claiming to be the son of Longabaugh. Personally, I can't completely discount this, he did know things that are not common knowledge, some of which had never been printed. For instance, he knew that Etta Place had been the second woman at the Roost, he knew where the cabin was on Fort Bottom on the Green River below Green River, Utah, and his claims that it was used by the Wild Bunch do not find me too much of a sceptic—there are a number of old names carved into the walls. Also, he knew of a shoot-out at the old Palmer House in Green River that is not common knowledge. After finding him right on the money with a few things, I didn't dare challenge him on anything, although some of his stories were a bit wild.

He said:

> . . . Yet these authors all quote Pinkerton's detective records as their authority. Yet Pinkertons admit that the last they knowed of them they were living in the southwest coast of Chile.
>
> I think some of these authors, including this University of Utah man has missed the boat. Funny part of it is the things that really happened from what my father and Butch have told me, they had stopped at this little barrio all right, to get something to eat. While they were there, two other American outlaws, a fellow by the name of Harry

I. V. Button, "the kid at the CS ranch," on Patsy, the horse given to him by Butch Cassidy. This picture was taken in 1909, when both were in their late teens.

—COURTESY OF I. V. BUTTON

LEFT: Harry Longabaugh, Jr., standing beside Joe Walker's grave in the Price, Utah, cemetery. He says he is the son of The Sundance Kid and Anna Marie Thayne from Castle Gate, half-sister of Etta Place. He claims that she was the school-teacher and Etta was just a dis-satisfied housewife. He says that he has a copy of the di-vorce papers, naming him as issue of the marriage.

(AUTHOR'S NOTE: Although Thayne is a common name in Carbon and Emery Counties, no record has so far been found by any of us that there was an Anna Marie Thayne.)

Nation and a man named Dick Clifford rode into the camp. Neither my father nor Butch liked either one of them, so they just hurried up and started to leave. Just down the street a short ways, when the gun battle broke loose, Dad and Butch were both hit by ricocheting bullets, but both survived. And they definitely were not in that actual gun battle, just in an aftermath of it.

Then the amusing part of this whole thing is, this Corregidor or local cop who first spotted them and went to get the cavalry, he and this cavalry officer got to fighting over who was going to collect the reward; got in a gun battle and both of them died as a result of the wounds they received in the gun battle, and the reward was never paid.

Whatever happened, it *is* certain that Butch Cassidy did return to the United States. In 1929 he visited his family in Circleville, and spent several days with them. He didn't want them to tell anyone about his being there, and they never did; even members of their own family didn't know about it.

He visited both in New Mexico and in Lander, and many, many old friends saw him. He is supposed to have died in the Northwest in either 1936 or 1937, and there is one story he is buried in Johnny, Nevada.

The Parker family in Circleville, Utah, have always been close-mouthed about him. I knew the family for years and finally became good friends with Lula Parker Betenson, Butch's sister. She tells me the reason the Parkers have always had nothing to say about Butch was not because they were ashamed of him, or because they didn't know anything—they got tired of being quizzed and having the credit (and the pay!) fall into someone else's hands.

Lula (past eighty, but plenty sharp) is now compiling a history of her interesting family, and plans to tell the true story of what happened to Butch in South America. Who can tell it better—particularly that part of it following the Castle Gate holdup—than the sister who was a baby the spring Butch left home?

THE CASTLE GATE
PAYROLL HOLDUP

The Castle Gate holdup of the Pleasant Valley Coal Company payroll was probably the most difficult job Butch Cassidy and Elzy Lay ever pulled. It was certainly the best planned. There were several hazards—the difficult terrain, the time of the robbery, with the risk of placing themselves on the ground without exciting suspicion looming the most important.

Castle Gate lies in the heart of the Carbon County coal empire in the bottom of the narrow gut of Price River Canyon. Highway and railroad fill almost all available space in the canyon for two or three miles below and above Castle Gate. The canyon walls are precipitous and, until they fall back and Gordon Creek enters from the south, there is little chance of emerging from the main gorge in a southeasterly direction.

The payroll came in on the noon train from Salt Lake City. While a train holdup along the line might have netted the cash, it seemed to the boys more feasible to wait until the paymaster had collected it and was carrying it to the coal company offices. These were located in the second story of the store building, reached by an outside stairway. It looked like the best strategy would be to relieve the paymaster of his baggage along the foot of the stairway.

The heist would have to be made in the midst of crowds of miners gathered to collect their pay. This meant, also, that not only would there be a good many people on the ground to see what was going on, but also that there would be a full staff in the offices. Lay figured the foot of the stairs was the easiest place to shield the scene of action, being against the building and the stairway.

The only transportation that could be used was horses. But horses were almost unknown in the crowded, narrow canyon, where it was difficult even to find room to set houses for the workers. The coal miners were mostly foreigners, anyway, and knew or cared little about horses. A man on a horse loomed up like a sore thumb, as Butch had expressed it.

The trick was to get the horses needed for a quick getaway and a long run, smuggled in some way that would not arouse suspicion. Riding boldly in wouldn't do, not on pay day, that is; particularly since James Smith, special officer for the Pleasant Valley Coal Company, had expressed his sentiments about the lax law enforcement by Sheriff Donant. Smith knew the Wild Bunch was ever present, that its members were competent and daring and that the Pleasant Valley Coal Company payroll was big enough to be a real temptation. Butch and Lay were well aware that James Smith, no fool by any means, was pretty much alert.

This problem of getting in inconspicuously had been hashed over numerous times the preceding winter. The best solution they had come up with was to take advantage of the horse-racing customs of the times. Race men rode their horses constantly to harden them, and these jockeys were to be seen almost anywhere. They had not been seen in the bottom of a narrow defile, without level ground enough for a race track in a hundred miles, but when two men came riding in without saddles, but with racing sur-

cingles, enough of the bystanders would have seen the sight
to allay suspicion.

On the day of the holdup, the two rode up to the store
just before train time. Butch dismounted and handed
the reins of the mare Babe to Lay, who was mounted on
the big brown horse, Kid. Butch stamped over to the building, kicked a box around to the wall where he could lean
back, and sat down, crossing his legs. He was the picture
of ease, lounging against the wall, swinging his booted foot
to hear his spurs jingle. It was plain to be seen he hadn't
a care in the world.

Lay sat on Kid, almost as relaxed, and the two horses,
at first restless among so many people in a strange place,
settled down and stopped fidgeting.

Much to Lay's relief, a native wandered out of the dark-
skinned crowd and, admiring the horses, started a conversation.

"Where you headed, mister?" he asked.

"Salt Lake City," Lay answered. "We've some races
matched there in a couple of weeks, and thought we'd take
it easy and mosey in."

"Looks like you got the horseflesh to get the job done,"
the miner agreed. "And you can't get a much finer finish
on them."

Lay started to sweat. The conversation was beginning
to get a little too technical. Last thing he needed was for
the condition of the two horses to get any notice. While
he was frantically trying to think of another topic, the
train whistle drifted in from up the canyon, and the miners
all turned away, their interests changing.

The paymaster, E. L. Carpenter, pattered down the
stairway in his bedroom slippers. He had a sore corn, and
had been wearing flapping bedroom slippers to work for
several days in the hope the tender toe would heal. He had
carried the payroll from the train to the office for years,
and saw no need to dress elaborately for the part.

Butch pulled back his foot to leave plenty of room for
the paymaster to get by. Carpenter trotted down to the
depot, collected a leather satchel and three sacks of coins
and came back. The men standing around had mostly

gone either into the store or down to the train. When Carpenter came back, he noticed the cowboy was still sitting at the foot of the stairs, and the horseman and two horses had moved in closer, but there was nothing to make him uneasy. He stepped past the horses, and the cowboy, and put his foot on the first step. All at once he felt a very near presence and a voice said very quietly, right in his ear, "I'll take that bag." Butch had risen suddenly, and had taken Carpenter so by surprise that he let the valise and money sacks be taken from him, through sheer shock.

Turning swiftly, Butch tossed two of the money sacks to Lay across Babe's head, and spooked her. Lay caught the bags, but Babe reared back, and jerked the reins out of his hand, and bolted down the canyon.

"Robbers!" yelled Carpenter, and raced up the stairs. Someone in the company offices grabbed a rifle kept there for protection, and started pumping lead from the office window.

Butch was hot after Babe, when Lay managed to out-maneuver her and crowd her into the railroad trestle. Slivers and dust were flying out of the timbers of the trestle by this time from the rifle slugs put there by the company marksman.

Babe eluded Elzy twice, but as she backed up when he headed her off, he reached and got the reins. Butch wasn't far behind and mounted the barebacked horse in one fluid swoop. Lay put spurs to Kid, and the terrified Babe fell behind to fly down the narrow canyon out of range of the rifle.

The money sacks were too cumbersome to hold, and the satchel was too obvious. Stopping behind a section house where they had cached their saddles, Butch and Lay quickly cut the satchel open and transferred the contents to a canvas bag they had brought along. The satchel held $7,000 in $20 gold pieces, and two of the sacks contained over $1,000 in silver and currency. Another sack held about $860 in small silver. This latter was just too heavy to handle, so they tossed it into the bed of a wagon they passed a few yards after stopping. In the few moments they were out of sight behind the section shack, and while they transferred the money and tied it in a slicker behind Lay's saddle, the engine passed them.

Carpenter, noting the buck-fever symptoms of the man with the rifle, turned and ran back down the stairs and to the depot. The closest law was in Price, about nine miles down the canyon. The station agent, wild-eyed, met Carpenter with the news the telegraph lines had been cut, and he couldn't get through to Price.

Being a man of action, Carpenter dashed out to the train, which was still at the depot, ordered the engine cut loose and swung up into the cab. The engineer opened the throttle, and away they raced. They were picking up speed when they passed Butch and Lay behind the section shack, and didn't see them. Before getting into Price, Carpenter tied down the whistle and when they screamed to a stop, the sheriff was already on hand, knowing something was wrong.

Butch and Lay, mounted up again, dashed down the canyon. They turned up Gordon Creek where the first relay was waiting at a ranch. Kid and Babe were badly winded, and the boys wasted no time changing to the new mounts.

Lay picked up Gray Eagle, and Butch transferred his saddle to a little bay horse belonging to Jack Moran. Babe and Kid were a shade faster than these two, but lacked their staying power—and there was a forty-mile run to Mexican Bend on the San Rafael. The race was slowed now, to conserve the strength of the horses. Mexican Bend lay below where the San Rafael cut through the Reef, at the end of a trail through some pretty rough country, desolate and rock strewn, with no chance to pick up a fresh mount along the way.

Crossing the road south of Price that led to the towns of Emery County—Huntington, Castle Dale, Cleveland, Orangeville—the two met the mail carrier. Mail was sent from the railroad to the outlying towns by packhorse, and these mail riders and pack strings were on the road all the time. They really knew who was traveling. This man had no way of knowing who the two strangers were, and they slowed while in his sight, lifted hands in a salute as they passed and went on.

In Price, Joe Walker had cut the telegraph wires at the exact time decided upon, after the train orders had gone through on the passenger train and before the holdup. He started back toward Miller Creek, south of Price, where he had stashed his outfit at a ranch. He planned to ride to Florence Creek, thinking it might not be well to linger in the area after the holdup.

When he heard the engine come screaming out of the canyon, he cursed. Some nosy official had thought of the only way to carry the message fast! Whipping up his horse, he paused only long enough at the ranch to change his saddle to the sorrel Whitmore horse. He lit a shuck to intercept the boys and tell them their time was even more limited than they thought. He debated making a detour west to cut the phone lines to Emery County, not knowing that Lay and Butch would do this, although too late to keep the message from going through. Posses were mounting up in Huntington and Castle Dale as soon, almost as those in Price.

Even as Joe headed out to intercept the boys, the posse from Price had met the mail carrier. He described their men, one of them about thirty-five years of age, and the other middle aged. The younger man wore a black hat, blue coat and goggles. (Why he added these, no one seems ever to have figured out.) Both men were sun-browned, and appeared more like cowboys, he said, than desperate highwaymen, although they were both carrying sixshooters. Not until he met the posse, did he know there had been a robbery.

Just below Desert Lake, Butch and Lay picked up a rider, trailing a plume of dust, cutting in from the side. Just before they figured to pull off and either ambush him, or elude him, they recognized Joe Walker.

"You boys have sure stirred up a hornets' nest," Joe said, as he rode up. They all trotted out, while he told them what he had been able to learn.

After discussion, the three decided that he should take the money and cut across country to Florence Creek, while they led the posse to the Roost.

"But look at your horse," Butch, ever the horseman,

said. "Sure am glad I took this Moran horse instead of that sorrel."

"I didn't save him any," Joe replied.

"Even at that, he shouldn't be in that kind of shape. It would take him a week to get to Florence Creek."

"Told you he wasn't the horse *that* one is," Joe agreed. "Guess I'll have to go back to Miller Creek and pick up another mount."

"Like hell you will!" Lay put in. "Not with our money! We'll let you take a horse from Mexican Bend. We've got an extra."

"What'll *you* do then?"

"If we don't have the money, they might not find it easy to convict us, even if they do catch us—and they won't," Butch answered. "I don't see them following us to the Roost."

It was just getting dark when they pulled into Mexican Bend, their horses pretty well used up. Butch pulled the shoes off the horse he had planned to ride from there, turned him over to Walker, and they changed the slicker-wrapped money to the back of his saddle. Joe mounted, and set off north across the country west of Green River, to hit Price River below Woodside. There he would go north to wait for them at Florence Creek—or Brown's Park if they didn't follow in the next day or two after leaving a plain trail to the Roost. A single, unshod track would never be noticed where Walker planned to ride.

The boys didn't have such outstanding horses at Mexican Bend. They had planned to use their best at first, and the wry joke they had made all winter was that if they still needed that kind of horses, it would be too late—a gentle packhorse and a bed roll to pack in their bodies would do as well. However, things were looking a little grim, and they wished for a better mount for Joe, as well as themselves.

Putting the boy who had been keeping the horse there for them on Gray Eagle, and handing him the lead rope of the Moran horse, they started him back up the country, telling him to be careful, but to go straight to the Moran ranch, and leave the horses there.

Butch mounted the boy's saddle horse, Lay stepped up on the one he had planned to ride, and they started off.

"What shall we do with this Whitmore horse?" the boy asked.

"Not a damn thing," Butch called back. "You don't know a thing about that horse, understand?"

A few days later Little Black Pete Jensen, a local farmer, found the horse and took it to his ranch. When the sorrel had rested up a bit, and started to look fat and sleek again, Black Pete went out to do the chores one morning and the horse was gone—through a closed gate.

The boys didn't take the Walker trail out of the canyon. Butch could tell before he had ridden a hundred yards that he needed a better horse. Down the river a rancher by the name of Halverson (the same rancher who was to loan Jack Moore the old sorrel horse) had a few head of horses, some pretty good ones the boys had noted.

About midnight the boys rode up, and the rancher got out of bed, dressed and came out to ask what they wanted. They were just pulling down the bars of the corral, and answered that they needed a horse, and asked him which was the best he had. He declined to comment, but the two went into the corral, struck a few matches and caught out the best horse there. The rancher, seeing it was a trade anyway, said he would take their horse and $20 to boot. Butch threw down $50, as Lay mounted, and they were off again.

The little black dog, Sunday, that they had enjoyed at the Roost, had followed them from Mexican Bend. That night he made it pretty well, since they stopped and rested for two or three hours toward morning.

The whole country back of them was up in arms. It had been decided that the Huntington posse was to go down Cottonwood Wash, but they fumbled around, and followed the tracks of the Castle Dale group down Buckhorn Canyon. Just at dusk they overtook the Castle Dale horsemen, and with each posse thinking that the other group was the outlaws, a battle was joined.

Pete Burson shot at Old Joe Meeks at fourteen steps with a double-barreled shotgun, and never even hit the horse. The Huntington bunch turned tail and ran, and someone shot a sorrel race mare named Pigeon, ridden by Little Joe Miller, wounding her in the stifle.

Hostilites ceased for a spell, and finally someone recognized a voice, and the parties got together, each bunch loath to admit they had been blasting away at each other —until they commenced comparing notes. Old Pete Burson said that one of the outlaws was packing a good load of buckshot; by the flash of his gun he could tell the target was a sandy-complected fellow, with a week's growth of beard. He lost considerable face as an outlaw exterminator when they proved to him it was Joe Meeks with a white beard a foot long.

A little gunpowder had cooled their ardor somewhat, and some of them found the dark of night anything but reassuring. Besides, the cows back home hadn't been milked.

The local men turned back but, after resting a while, Joe Bush and a few more pushed on, coming at daylight out onto the desert. They soon picked up the outlaws' tracks, and after swinging along for a mile or two, caught sight of their quarry. But they didn't close in too fast, being careful to stay out of gunshot range.

As the hot April morning wore along on the sandy desert, Sunday lippety-lipped along, his tongue hanging farther out, and his beloved Butch drawing farther and farther ahead. Finally Sunday had fallen so far behind he was following the posse, and even way behind them.

Butch looked back, and saw the tiny black dot moving along in the distance. "That dog has stayed with us better than most men," he declared.

"So what?" Lay answered.

"So you mosey along up onto that ridge and play that posse some Winchester music. I'll drop down this draw, cross behind that knoll down there, pick up Sunday, come back the same way and join you. Now don't be too eager, and shoot too damn close, and run them back over me. Just halt them."

Butch reached the little black dog without accident, and while he heard with glee a few shots up ahead, dropped down the draw and rode up behind the ridge to join Lay. Shortly after that they turned off toward the Flat Tops, and the posse of Joe Bush, Pete Anderson and Floyd of Castle Gate, George Whitmore, a fellow from Provo, and Carpenter turned back. Carpenter was still wearing his bedroom slippers, never having found time to locate his shoes.

The posse missed the bunch from Green River under L. S. Dickerson of Salt Lake City, who went out the Hanksville road. The mail carrier to Hanksville was returning from there, and reluctantly told them he had seen the outlaws, traveling pertly along. The posse decided it was useless to follow them on jaded (?) horses.

After a few days at the Roost, Lay and Butch wandered into Hanksville to see what was being said about the

Butch Cassidy's name carved in a sloping sandstone ledge. Noel Baker, son of the author, points to the weathered name and to a date. The name is almost obliterated, while the date is plain and sharp, indicating that it was carved much later.

—PHOTO BY PEARL BAKER

holdup. Excitement had died down, but there were some dandy stories making the rounds.

One such story was that they had taken a mare and colt up on the mountain above Huntington, and left the colt in a corral up there. The mare they took to Castle Gate, loaded the loot on her and turned her loose. Naturally, she went right back to her colt, where an accomplice of the robbers took care of her pack. Butch used to remark in later years it was a damn good idea, and he wished he'd thought of it.

Another story originated with the Emery County possemen. It concerned how closely the boys were pressed on the road from Price to Cleveland. It seems Butch's horse kept lagging back, and finally Lay turned in his saddle and wanted to know what was the reason.

"It's this damn silver," Butch was supposed to have said. "It weighs ten pounds, and it slows us down."

"Throw the damn stuff away," Lay reportedly advised. "We can't fool around with that, and take a chance on getting caught."

"I've been trying to, but my saddle strings have pulled down so tight I can't get the knot untied."

"Here, I'll show you how to fix that." And Lay got his pocket knife out and, as Butch came up alongside, reached over and slit the bottom of the sack. Silver dollars sprayed down the road for half a mile, and were picked up by a farmer in a wagon.

And then there was that pair of goggles!

A few days later Butch and Lay traveled north again, picking up Kid, Gray Eagle and Babe from near Price. Heading down the Price River and up the Green, they crossed at the mouth of Florence Creek and went on to Brown's Park.

Many people thought for years that the Castle Gate loot was buried at the Roost. While it was never taken there, other hauls were. And it is not impossible that there are still buried caches in the canyons or on the mesas of that fabulous country. The men who might have returned for them are all dead now, but a few years ago a cache *was* retrieved—by a man who knew exactly where he was going!

Crow Seep Ranch headquarters at the time the author ran the ranch at Robbers Roost.

—PHOTO COURTESY OF RICHARD BEDIER, GREEN RIVER, UTAH

The author, at the age of 25, when she was personally managing The Roost.

—PHOTO FROM PEARL BAKER

CACHES AT
THE ROOST

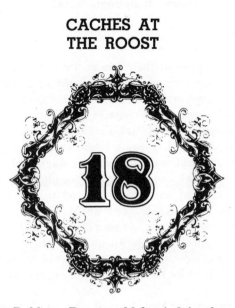

Is there any Robbers Roost gold buried in those badlands, blind canyons, hidden parks and windswept mesas where Butch Cassidy and his Wild Bunch returned after pulling a holdup? The arguments have raged for years, but Andy Moore * added a little information to the controversy a

---

* North Springs, a relatively big spring for this country, lies north of the Roost, in the middle of what is loosely called the San Rafael Desert. Bill Tomlinson, who lived at the Roost as a child, started a cow outfit there, but because there were no natural barriers to contain his herd, found it was not a good layout; while he was digging a cow out of the mud on the Dirty Devil River, two more were dying in the mud of the San Rafael. His family was getting up to school age, and his wife hated the desert. He pulled out and the North Springs country lay "open" for a few years, until McMullin brought in several hundred head of yearling steers to overrun and take possession of the country from the San Rafael River to the breaks of the Colorado—including Robbers Roost.

Andy Moore was his foreman, but there were never enough men to take care of the steers, and they drifted down onto points looking off into canyons or the rivers and choked to death; local ranchers took their toll in beef, and the whole deal collapsed.

Andy could see, however, that if a man wanted to spend all his time with his outfit, he could develop a spread at North Springs, and he moved in with a few cows and calves in the early 1920s. He "coyoted" it (lay out with not much camp, and very little food, living a very rough life) for some years, and did make a go of it, leaving a good outfit when he died a few years ago. This story occurred during his early years when he was living in the cabin that Tomlinson had built at Twin Springs, around the ridge from North Springs.

few years ago:

> I was camped at the cabin at Twin Springs along about
> 1930, before I moved the cabin south of North Springs. It
> set then about seven or eight miles north of North Springs,
> and back against the ridge.
>
> One evening about dark a stranger rode up the draw. He
> seemed surprised to see a house there, and to find some-
> one around, but was agreeable to staying all night. I had
> been awful sick and was glad to see him.
>
> He unpacked and unsaddled and turned his horses up
> over the point where they would probably run into my
> bunch when they got far enough to hear the bell on mine.
> We had supper and redded up the dishes, then started to
> go to bed. He didn't have a bed, said he had figured to
> sleep out here by the spring, so, of course, he bunked with
> me.
>
> He was slower than I to get undressed, so when I rolled
> into bed he blew out the lamp. I could hear a shoulder
> holster squeak when he pulled off his shirt, but I always let
> a feller's garb be his own business, so I didn't pay any
> attention if he took the gun off when he went to bed. Prob-
> ably did, though, and hung it on the bedstead.
>
> I had to get up and go out in the night, and he got up,
> too. Stood in the door near where he'd piled his pack outfit
> until I came in.
>
> The next morning I was some better, but still felt tough,
> and while this jasper was no talker, I didn't hurry around
> to get the horses to get him on his way. He didn't seem in
> a hurry, either, although he acted nervous, especially when
> I happened to get near his pack outfit. Finally, I could
> see he wasn't going after the horses, so I took my bridle
> and started out. His horse and mule were with mine, and I
> brought them in.
>
> He saddled up, and when I offered help in packing his
> mule, he refused it and threw the diamond hitch by him-
> self. I grained my horses, but I still felt too puny to work
> that day, so kept up a horse and turned the rest back up
> over the point. The fellow pulled out after thanking me for
> my hospitality, and I went back into the cabin to rest
> awhile.

The more I thought about the way he had acted, the curiouser I got about the whole affair. If I had been myself, I would have noticed it before, but now I looked back, I got to wondering why he was so careful not to let me get near the pack.

About noon I felt a little better, and saddled up to take the fellow's back trail and find out where he had been. I found he had gone past Twin Spring on the way in, and headed straight for North Springs. Here, he had watered his horses, then gone back down the canyon about a quarter of a mile where there is a little cave up on the canyon wall. He'd tied his horses to a catclaw bush, and climbed to the cave. Tracks in the sand at the bottom of the sloping wall showed plain where he had taken his boots off and left them there, climbing the slope in his sock feet. It's too steep to climb any other way, and I followed his example.

In the sand of the cave floor was a hole about three feet deep and a couple of feet across. Something had been dug up, carried down the cliff and loaded onto the pack mule.

I was really interested now, and the next morning I took his trail toward San Rafael. Wasn't long until he dropped into his outward trail, and the two sets of tracks made straight across the desert, crossing the San Rafael above the Gillies ranch. This was where oldtimers tell me the trail used by the Robbers Roosters used to cross the desert. We don't use that route at all, going by way of the mouth of Dugout or Tanks-of-the-Desert. But Butch and his gang had a trail, long ago wiped out by the desert wind, that this fellow took.

When I inquired in Green River, I found he had come in on the train, hired this horse and mule from Frank Howlett, neither asked nor answered any questions, returned the horses in a couple of days and left on the train.

Maybe there's no loot buried at the Roost now, but I believe the time was when I could have reached out and touched some that had been buried there.

And I, when I was a child, have taken off my boots so that I could climb that same steep wall without slipping, and have run up to that little cave and played around in it many times.

There is also the story that two fellows rode into Thompson the day after Flat Nose George was killed. The rumor got around that they had come there to split up $65,000 that Flat Nose had for safekeeping. They quietly disappeared, but the rumor remained, known to few—but still around.

A few years later Bill Brock moved into the area and bought a ranch at Green River. He was a local man, having had a ranch in Nine Mile, above Price, before coming to Green River. He had heard the rumor and spent days and days from time to time hunting the cave where Flat Nose had stayed the winter before he was killed. This was during the time that Budge Wilcox's father was running cattle in Rattlesnake. They knew he was hunting a treasure of some kind, but they didn't know where the cave was, either.

Several years later, after Brock had been long dead, Budge stumbled onto the cave while hazing a cow out of the brush on the hillside. But practical stockmen don't believe in buried treasure. That doesn't alter the fact, however, that Andy Moore says there was one, and who knows—perhaps there is more.

INDEX

Donant, Gus, 48, 202
Douglas Creek, 116
Dowd and Forrester, 82, 89
Dry Fork, Utah, 61
Dugout (at Roost), 37
Dugout (at San Rafael), 215
Duncan, Tap, 106, 107
Durango, Colorado, 58

Eagle City, 36
Eastern Utah Advocate, 77
Ekker, Arthur, 20, 28, 60
Ekker, Neilus, 53
Elko, Nevada, 100, 195
Elks Magazine, 105
Elliot, Scott, 91
Emery County, Utah, 163, 206, 211
England, 181
Enoch Train, 182
Evanston, Wyoming, 82

Fairview, 30, 31
Farlow, Ed, 197
Farmers & Merchants Bank (See Delta Bank)
Farr, Sheriff, 176, 177
Farrer, Harry and Tom, 114
Farrers' Store, 39
Fausetts, 81
Ferron, Utah, 122, 124
Fisher Mesa, 160
Fish Lake, 19
Fitzpatrick, 193
Flat Nose George (See Curry)
Flat Tops, Utah, 124, 209
Florence Creek, Utah, 67, 69, 78, 85, 94, 206, 207, 211
Folsom, New Mexico, 107, 176, 189
Forest Lawn Cemetery, 180
Fort Bottom, 198
Fort Bridger, 64
Fort Duchesne, 129
Fort Worth, Texas, 105, 193
Foy, Tom, 121
Fremont County, Wyoming, 187
French, Captain, 174, 175, 176, 189
Fruen, 186
Fruita, Utah, 20, 116
Fullerton, 86, 88

Gale Undertaking Parlors, 168
Garnet Mesa, Colorado, 169
Gentry, Jack, 77
Gibbons, Ben, 41
Gibbons, Charles, 137
Gillette, Wyoming, 100
Gillies, Ann, 181, 184
Gillies, Dan, 187
Gillies, Ebb, 45
Gillies Ranch, 215
Gillies, Robert, 184
Glass, 196
Golconda, 192
Golden Stairs, 103
Goodman, 111
Gordon Creek, Utah, 201
Gordon, W. E. (Latigo), 135, 146
Grand Junction, Colorado, 30, 39, 85, 134
Grand River, 154, 163
Grand Valley Times, 145, 147
Granite, 40, 42, 43, 70, 114
Granite Wash, 30, 36
Grass Valley, 19, 30
Green River, 13, 23, 27, 41, 56, 67, 78, 82, 86, 100, 115, 171, 211
Green River, Utah, 13, 19, 20, 40, 44, 46, 47, 64, 67, 100, 103, 114, 125, 135, 156, 207, 210
Griffith, John (Blue John), 44, 131, 172, 174
Grimes, 36, 41, 109, 116
Grimes, Gene, 149
Grimes, Howard, 157
Griswold's Second Hand Store, 167
Gunnison River, 169

Hainer, Al, 186
Halverson, Chris, 42, 44, 136, 208
Hamilton, Parker, Mrs., 60
Hammel, Jim, 134
Hammond, 167
Hancock, Sheriff, 145, 148
Hanks, Charl, 144
Hanks, Neil, 35, 36, 38, 117
Hanksville, Utah, 17, 30, 31, 34, 36, 40, 42, 53, 65, 96, 114, 125, 135, 137, 144, 210
Hart Draw, 121

Runt's Knob, 172

Sabey, Alice, 55
Sacramento, California, 191
Salina, 67, 114, 116, 151
Salt Lake City, Utah, 50, 61, 89, 101, 123, 179, 201, 210
San Augustin Plains, 175
San Domingo Mine, 195
Sanford, Gene, 36, 41, 43
San Miguel County, Colorado, 158
San Miguel Valley Bank, 159
San Rafael Desert, 27, 30, 40, 41, 69, 70, 115, 123, 213
San Rafael River, 27, 42, 44, 69, 136, 172, 213, 215
San Rafael Swell, 21, 76
Santa Fe, 178
San Vicente, 196
Saunders, B. F., 121
Sawtooth Range, 102
Scipio, 78
Scott, Len, 111
Seattle, Washington, 108
Seibert, 195
Sevier River, 21
Shadron, Nebraska, 94, 104
Shaughnessy, Mike, 186
Shoot-'Em-Up-Bill, 53
Shoshoni, Wyoming, 132
Shultz, Mizzoo, 81
Silver Reef, 184
Silver Tip (See Wall, Bill)
Silver Tip Spring, 33, 38, 140
Simms, Joe (See Parker, Dan)
Simpson, W. Ray, 166
Sinbad, Colorado, 149, 169
Sinbad, Utah, 53
Smith, J. L., 48, 49, 202
Smith, Tom, 177
Soldier's Pass, 192
South America, 93, 97, 105, 108, 176, 186, 194, 199
South Dakota, 97
Spanish-American War, 77
Spanish Bottom, 118, 143
Spanish Trail, 118
Speck, 98, 100
Spicer, 44
Springer, New Mexico, 176
Springville Bank, Utah, 50

Spur, 23
Starr, Al, 23, 122, 123
Star Valley, 58
Staunton, Dick, 62
Staunton, Ike, 62
Steele, Mike, 182
Stoddard, Rufe, 42, 70, 123
Stony Creek, 160
Straight Wash, 41, 122
Strawberry, 56
Strip, 129
Sundance Kid, the (See Longa-baugh)
Sunday, 39, 117, 208
Sunnyside, 86, 89, 91
Sunset Pass, 118
Swasey, 174
Swasey's Leap, 71
Sweetwater, 125
Switzerland, 40
Sylvester, Joe, 33

Tall Texan (See Kilpatrick)
Tangren, Andrew, 145
Tanks-of-the-Desert, 215
Taylor Brothers, 111, 134, 162
Taylor, Crip, 104
Taylor, Don, 162
Taylor, Frank, 63
Taylor, Jick, 162
Taylor, Joseph, 135
Taylor, Lester, 162
Telluride, 17, 18, 24, 27, 41, 57, 58, 121, 122, 157, 158, 162, 185
Telluride Bank (San Miguel Bank), 58, 64, 162
Temple Mountain, 41, 114
Tennessee, 152
Texas, 35, 37, 45, 66, 68, 85, 134
Texas Rangers, 36
Thayne, Anna Marie, 199
Thayne, Edgar, 48
Thermopolis, Wyoming, 100
Thompson, Ott, 146
Thompson, Sant, 81
Thompson Springs, 68, 81, 82, 88, 94, 174, 216
Thompson, Wim, 41, 113, 121
Thousand Lake Mountains, 30
Three-B Outfit, 27, 29, 35, 38, 40, 41, 44, 133

223

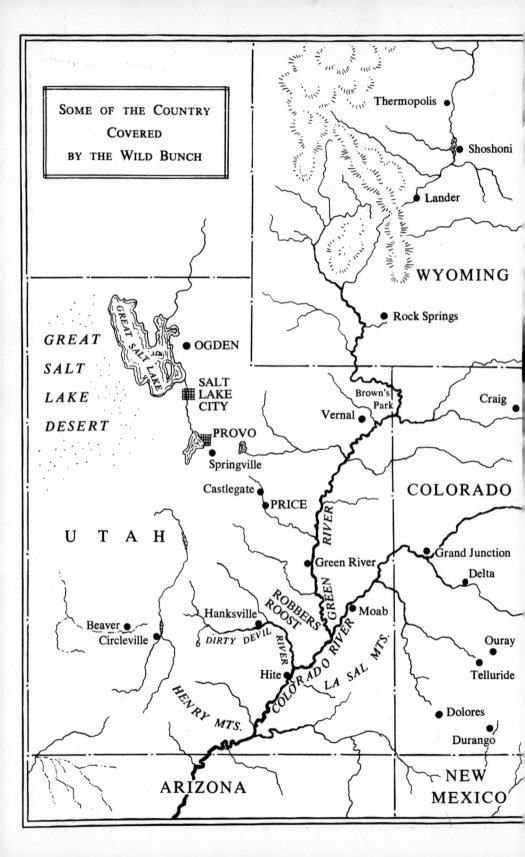

SOME OF THE COUNTRY
COVERED
BY THE WILD BUNCH